Please renew or return items by the date shown on your receipt

www.hertfordshire.gov.uk/libraries

Renewals and enquiries: 0300 123 4049

Textphone for hearing or 0300 123 4041
speech impaired users:

L32 11.16

Hertfordshire

PARENTS

an anthology of poems by women writers

Edited by

Myra Schneider and Dilys Wood

Preface by U. A. Fanthorpe

London
ENITHARMON PRESS
2000

First published in 2000
by the Enitharmon Press
36 St George's Avenue
London N7 0HD

Distributed in Europe
by Littlehampton Book Services
through Signature Book Representation
2 Little Peter Street
Manchester M15 4PS

Distributed in the USA and Canada
by Dufour Editions Inc.
PO Box 449, Chester Springs
PA 19425, USA

ISBN 1 900564 71 8

British Library Cataloguing-in-Publication Data.
A catalogue record for this book is available
from the British Library.

The Enitharmon Press gratefully acknowledges a grant from the
London Arts Board towards the production costs of this volume.

Set in Bembo by Bryan Williamson, Frome,
and printed in Great Britain by
The Cromwell Press, Wiltshire

Contents

THREE BOTH PARENTS

Preface

I suppose many people, if asked what is the greatest theme of poetry, would say *Love*, or *Time*. It seems clear to me, faced with this fine anthology, that the right answer is *Parents*. For parents combine love and time, and in a very striking, difficult way. The love is often embarrassed, undeclared, too late − tangled in some way. And the time is reversed; the parent is the child, the child the parent, by the processes of time. So it certainly is here, where the older women see elderly parents as their children; remember the energy and passion of parents who were younger than they are now; or recall their younger, brusque or uncomprehending selves. The originality of combining the theme with the special insights of women, who are often more vulnerable to their parents than their brothers are, and also less able to escape, adds to the particular qualities of this anthology.

The age of the poets is important, too. It's strange to think that, not so long ago, poets were expected to die before they were thirty, or else to experience a geriatric late flowering. We can see now how such expectations limited the scope of poetry. Those who have lived hardest and thought most deeply are not generally the under-thirties, who haven't seen all that much of it, or the very old, whose perspectives are blurred by nostalgia. It's the women, the Second Light Network, who have seen, but have often been stifled, who are speaking out now, with anger, despair, pathos, wit, love, cunning. This anthology has brought some of them together.

Read. They will amaze you.

U. A. FANTHORPE

Foreword

The remarkable emergence of women's poetry in the last twenty years has coincided with a much greater openness in discussing feelings. One of the strengths of this poetry is its perceptive exploration of complex relationships. This is very evident in the way women examine the link or lack of it between themselves and their parents at different stages of their lives and in the way they trace changing perspectives when they become their ageing parents' carers. We therefore welcomed Enitharmon's interest in the idea of an anthology of poems which would include some of the best work by living women poets on the theme of parents.

We found a wealth of exciting material to choose from by well-known and new poets. We have included poems that celebrate love as well as explorations of ambivalent feelings, dramatic presentations of damaging relationships and expressions of anger. The work in the book also focuses on parents' lives, their attitudes, relationships with one another, their ageing and dying.

The contributors live in Britain though several of them were born in other countries. They are people from very different backgrounds with varied experiences of life. Most of them were born before 1960 and a number of poems reflect the social life of the 1940s and 1950s. Several refer to major wars. There are moving poems by refugees whose parents were taken away by the Nazis, about a father who fought in the Spanish Civil War, about parents who were imprisoned during Stalin's purges and the words of a father re-living his experiences on the Somme during his last illness. Some writers reflect growing up in wartime Britain. Others relate extraordinary events in their parents' early lives, a few use fairy tale to depict destructive relationships. There is a phone call to a stepmother, a dialogue with a father after his death, a description of bathing a dependent mother, a search for a birth mother. The poems are in a variety of styles and tones: tender, angry, questioning, meditative, conversational, humorous.

In preparing this anthology we have drawn on the support of the Second Light Network of older women poets whose aims include the promotion of women's writing, both members' and non members'. This fast-growing organisation is for women poets aged about forty

11

and over who are widely published or beginning to be so. It has a regular newsletter and offers opportunities for readings, publication, workshops and the exchange of ideas.

MYRA SCHNEIDER
DILYS WOOD

MOTHERS

To My Mother

You made the home where I go home in dream.
There, I'm a child coming out of the sun
into the shady kitchen where you sit
turning sheets 'sides to middles'. Your machine
is singing like grasshoppers on the common.
Perhaps you're making me that yellow dress
I wore through several Summers. Happiness
is yellow like that dress, or like the sun.
Where rabbits on the common dig the sand
their warren's yellow, like a splash of light,
even on greyest days when rains repress
the shining of the cheerful dandelion.
Piano scales sound from the sitting-room;
my father batters typewriter upstairs.
Outside his workroom window, while he turns
his talent to commodity, he sees
the lesbian passion of those years stride past
with setters on a leash. (This yet unknown.)
Outside, I have been loitering to define
elusive fragrances, considering
the creeping speedwell and the pimpernel,
the bindweed trumpets and the nightshade hats,
how weeds were dressed.
For me that garden was a kind of Eden.
You had a way of letting us be idle –
staring at lilies and pond-tortoises –
you didn't rush out with a shining needle
to make each minute useful. 'Practical',
from you, was critical. You had a gift
for words, one at a time, bearing great weight.
You had a gift for poetry, I thought;
when you were old you wrote
'I carry still-unwritten poems about',
but then it was too late.
You staked yourself on us: your husband too.
Our childhood was the meaning of your life.
You gave us freedom, and no book was hidden;
only becoming an adult was forbidden.

ANNA ADAMS

midwife

my mother was my midwife
she delivered me to a cold place
the internment planet
where no water runs

I heard her voice far off
beating at me to push and push.
I tried and failed, and failed
against the water's drag

sweetly she tripped me
out of Eden. the rocks pile up
as cold as breasts.
and I loved her

JUDITH KAZANTZIS (1977)

Mother, Dear Mother

She is invigilator; her name is knife.
She changes nappies and sleeps in my father's bed.

If I cry blazes or trickle, she'll come to my whistle
And give me her breast. Or let me lie and cry.

Half of her's mine, and half is my hot fat father's.
To each, one arm, one eye – and then what?

What is the good of possessing half a woman?
I'll pull her down to me by her swinging hair

And eat her all up, moon-face, belly and toes,
And throw the skin to my father, to keep him warm.

ELMA MITCHELL

17

Praise Song for My Mother

You were
water to me
deep and bold and fathoming

You were
moon's eye to me
pull and grained and mantling

You were
sunrise to me
rise and warm and streaming

You were
the fishes red gill to me
the flame tree's spread to me
the crab's leg/the fried plantain smell
                    replenishing replenishing

Go to your wide futures, you said

GRACE NICHOLS

The Woman Who Drank Us Up

She was the woman who drank us up,
gripped us in her graveyard clasp and drained us,
until we were almost uncreated, loose skin and slack bones.

She was the woman who smeared our lids with honey
until blisters, sugar pink and sweet the way she liked, frosted views,
extinguished stars, volcanoes, whole shining landscapes.

Each day, we were lifted to her lips, a flawless set, to be unfilled,
she swallowed us, the bitter juices, iron blood, the frothy head,
savoured her duty in the way that martyrs nurse small flames.

She was the woman who pulled down moons to make candles,
pressed them in hot wax to lock in light,
who even sipped the perfect dark of dreaming.

LESLEY QUAYLE

Griselda

Griselda stands at the window
in bitter cold.
She sees her mother, in firelight,
singing a doll to sleep.

The doll has Griselda's face.

The frost bites to the bone.
'Mother,' cries Griselda,
'mother, let me in!'

Her mother, moving quietly,
lays the doll to rest,
smoothes the coverlet,
turns down the light.

'Mother,' cries Griselda,
'let me in!'

What is this face at the window?

'Go away, ragged girl,' says her mother.
'Can't you see my child is asleep?'

EVANGELINE PATERSON

Ingredients of Glass

I am told
she dare not exclaim
her thoughts when she found me
busy at the pine table
building a tower
with best crystal
inherited from her mother.

Kept in the dresser
to be admired
when relatives gathered
on those rare occasions
betrothals, birthdays,
arrivals, departures.
A family like
the ingredients of glass
plain, useful, workaday:
the scrubbed harshness of skin
magnified through the transparency
of fragile goblets,
and the spun silicone
of their conversation
was blown into promises.
Whilst the lemonade
poured from an earthenware pitcher
and punch graced the mixing bowl,
our hands globed pottery mugs.

My tower grew tall
as her knuckles whitened.
I dismantled it, my touch
fine as blown ash.
She stood me on a stool
beside the sink
and dredging glass from the suds
held each to the light
that I might share
their circumference of rainbows.

MARGARET SPEAK

The Telling Part

Ma mammy bot me oot a shop
Ma mammy says I was a luvly baby

Ma mammy picked me (I wiz the best)
your mammy had to take you (she'd no choice)

Ma mammy says she's no really ma mammy
(just kid on)

It's a bit like a part you've rehearsed so well
you can't play it on the opening night
She says my real mammy is away far away
Mammy why aren't you and me the same colour
    But I love my mammy whether she's real or no
My heart started rat tat tat like a tin drum
all the words took off to another planet
Why

But I love ma mammy whether she's real or no

I could hear the upset in her voice
I says *I'm not your real mother*
though Christ knows why I said that
If I'm not who is, but all my planned speech
went out the window

    She took me when I'd nowhere to go
    my mammy is the best mammy in the world OK

After mammy telt me she wisnae my real mammy
I was scared to death she was gonnie melt
or something or mibbe disappear in the dead
of night and somebody would say she wis a fairy
godmother. So the next morning I felt her skin
to check it was flesh, but mibbe it was just
a good imitation. How could I tell if my mammy
was a dummy with a voice spoken by someone else
So I searches the whole house for clues
but I never found nothing. Anyhow a day after
I got my guinea pig and forgot all about it.

I always believed in the telling anyhow.
You can't keep something like that secret
I wanted her to think of her other mother
out there thinking that child I had will be
seven today eight today all the way up to
god knows when. I told my daughter –
I bet your mother's never missed your birthday
How could she?

JACKIE KAY

Another Kind of Skin

You had a skirt with flounces;
Scenes from *My Fair Lady*,
That gathered to your slim waist,
Laid youth on your child-bearing frame.

Your domestic routines were like
Miniature seasons: Mondays
Washing, Tuesdays ironing,
Wednesdays – the big bake.

One summer day you came
Out to the garden. Look, you said,
And spread before us
Manicured nails, brightly painted red.

Your skirt with its pictures
Blew in the breeze,
You displayed your fingers
As though your behaviour was risky –

A sudden unveiling of woman –
Not for the likes of a mother
With three growing children.

FRANCES SACKETT

My Mother's Clothes

The air was full of Gitane Filtre, her reflection

transformed by the spray that lifts from torrents,
the wardrobe door open, her clothes pristine.

Some were in polythene, preserved in the mist
from the day they were worn; a blue and peach suit

striped with Iceland's primeval landscape
where fire and ice hiss under Northern Lights.

She told me about her year in the Indian Embassy,
unwrapped a sari deep as the Gokak Falls,

charged with rust-red debris. Its many mirrors
retained faces of her admirers.

Right at the back, trailing along the wardrobe floor,
her bridal-dress was a river shot with scales of salmon.

Next were négligés, subterranean springs
cascading down slopes of mountains,

then a dressing-gown which towered in the frosty depths,
its cataract of ice fastening at her throat;

an emerald trouser-suit with matching silk blouse
was a secret chute from the South of France

where she'd tried to make us a home.
I fondled the ruff, its underwood trickle.

After that, there were no more choice materials,
only dull tweeds, sober crêpes for the mature woman,

modest falls in the Welsh hills where she'd settled.

PASCALE PETIT

natural high

my mother is a
red
woman

she
gets high
on clean children

grows
common sense

injects
tales
with heroines

fumes
over dirty habits

hits the sky
on bad lines

cracking meteors

my mother
gets red
with the sun

JEAN BINTA BREEZE

Woman Washing

At the side
of the porcelain sink
is a cracked jug.

Her thumb splays
across its surface
as she lifts it, bends forward

and thrusts the warm water
over her hair, rubs in the shampoo.
Violets this week.

Makes a great froth
on the top of her head
as she knuckles the lather.

Then three filled jugs
till all runs smooth and black.
Straightens, half naked.

I could swing from the strong balance
of her arms as she rubs and turbans
the towel about her.

Now fresh water
and face to waist
lathered and washed.

I think she must be beautiful.
Finger my own white dress
with the rabbits.

Rub a tuck of its cotton
against the smooth silk of her blouse,
gently touch the lines of stitches,

till she suddenly turns and I step back.
'Leave it alone' she says,
but not shouting.

PATRICIA BISHOP

Fitting

The Spirella lady sipped tea
from our thin china.
The cake
stayed on the trolley.
Perfectly still
on the settee
I wasn't offered any.

She opened her case.
Shook out tissue-wrapped
biscuit-pink cambric.

And mother stood shy
without her clothes
in the middle of the afternoon
her crossed arms dressing
her ample flesh
long laced
curvaceous
waisted
stayed.

Round her bottom
chubby suspenders
dangling free on her fat thighs
and over the top
her pinched back spilling
like cream in the cake
when she cut it.

PAULINE PRIOR-PITT

With my mother, missing the train

I remember being late. At the final minute
we'd run for the city train, which roared on past,
its line of faces scanning us not in it.
The air itself was roaring and the blast
of hot departed wheels embraced my mother,
crushing her flustered skirts into a flurry
with me there, clinging. 'Hush, there'll be another,'
she always reassured. 'No need to hurry.'
But there was a need. The speed of things was true
and the rush of traffic urged us both ahead.
I wanted to race again, to burst right through
and make the great train wait. She never said
that missing things was serious, yet her sighing
swept us on and up, hands fast, flying.

HELENA NELSON

My Exorcist Mother

'Do you know a dark man?'
I can hear it now
that gentle unassuming tone,
and the flip of cards
shuffled, cut, shuffled again.

They always brought their own,
why, I never really knew,
pulled discreetly out of shopping bags
about halfway through tea.

No one seemed to notice me
hovering under her arm,
with the pictures that went with the story
in bright rows under my chin,
or else gazing over her shoulder
into a teacup at a future
all there in black and white.

At the sight of a drip in the cup
after the ritual twist and drain,
the words, 'I see a few tears, Florence'
(or Nellie or Jane)
could choke up a story long held in.

She'd never lay cards for me;
you don't for your own, she'd say
and besides, what if she turned up spades?

With the tea-leaves I was indulged,
assured a brilliant future, even shown
some of the signs, though barely enough –
my exorcist mother insisted
you had to have the 'eye'.

PATRICIA ADELMAN

Handnotes

My mother hated gesturing. My speech
was always reinforced by hands, made concrete
by the shapes I drew in air.

So mother found my talk embarrassing,
her Puritan ancestors stronger than she knew,
no mother of her own to play the fingergames
small children use to reinforce
the wordspace time eventually fills.

But when I'd grown, and matched my growing with
a lexical increase, my fingers too
grew fluent, so a sort of doublespeak
emerged, language complete with detailed handnotes.

'Frills', mother would scoff. Seeing her real discomfort,
I would try mental straitjacketing, arms tight to sides.
Five minutes, max, and then, wild animals constrained
by sheltering, they'd twitch, too curious for caution.

It would be good to take my mother's hand again
and talk, get down to feelings once too near the bone.

LYN MOIR

Mother

1.
She asked for bread,
my grandmother gave a stone.

This was a child
on the edge of darkness,
who followed
the string to the heart
of the maze,

found
love at its source

which fed her to the son.

She was required
to smile
as she was consumed;

this was her gift.

2.
Silences
between us like
black owls asleep

we smile
across quiet talons,
feather on feather
trapping soft darkness.

Images of blood
and tearing
make us fear to wake
these birds
that eat our light.

They hunt in dreams.

If I could speak,
I would ask
why there is always a child
crying in my head.

I remember my father's
whip of words,
but you are nebulous,
bright but insubstantial;

I needed you solid as bread.

3.
My mother took
my skin
to wrap my sister in,

I grew
another that was new
and very thin;

she gave that too.

4.
We step round
holes in conversations,
talk of weather,
shopping, cutting grass,
words unequivocal
as cups of tea.

Our true language
has no voice,
fills rooms with ghosts,
dark, ungraspable
shapes
with damaging smiles.

These live
in gesture and look,
have laid down
strata made from bones
of tiny rages,
puzzlement, love;

grist for future deserts,
veins of dust?

ISOBEL THRILLING

Hansel and Gretel

They were not the abandoned ones,
the babes in the wood,
expiring blackberry-stained
under blankets of leaves.

No, they were the cherished ones,
the devoured ones,
fattened for the witch's table,
'parental love' a sugar house to trap them,
the hospitable oven meant for them.

He, with the sweetest flesh
being male, was gorged on witch-bait, caged
for the first kill.
She starved on oyster shells.

There was no come-back this time.

She died a skeleton, he grossly fat.

The Mother, left alone, a tragic figure
wears black now
licks the bones.

BARBARA NOEL-SCOTT

Old Stone Age

Sometimes she climbed
into my bed
in the dark back bedroom
with the half-finished bathroom
dad had been building
before he left.
She laid her head
on my chest.
Her hair tickled my mouth.
I could smell her white skin
Woodbine smoke
in her hair
whiskey fumes
on her breath
as she wept.
The thin straps
of her slip
left deep red welts
on her shoulders
like the welts she left
on our bodies
when we were small children.
I was older.
She needed me
child–become–mother
hunter–gatherer.
When she slept
I rose from the bed
leaving her curled
like an infant
the blanket
to her chin.
I'd enter the difficult world
and fend for her
using my wits

the way long ago
the first people
set out to pit themselves
against their quarry.

FRANCES ANGELA

Stepmother

Me she hated
without rhyme or reason.
She wedded my dad
when I was ten.
I couldn't win.
Nothing I did
altered
her goddess condemnation.
In painful fear
I avoided her,
responded
with hate I hid.

Now I know
she's a parasitical,
cruel illiterate.
At thirty four I still
redden and tremble,
back in that state,
reverberate:
Bad and small,
when I telephone
my father and: 'Her again,'
she whinnies down the hall,
'that loopy gal.'

DINAH LIVINGSTONE (1977)

In the Room I *

Come too late to see
the eyes someone's
thumbed shut.
Anger like shutters
slamming,
pity slicking the throat,
the nasal membrane swells,
oozes; tears are furious
hot.
Not for her. She's gone.
This one's for me.
That dreadful shift of face
from quick to this,
to dirty tallow,
yolk-eyes filmed over
by solid cataracts of skin,
these cheeks landslipped
from nose, no lips,
under the tautened sheet
how flat, how shrunk –
blown shell, husk.
Windows shut. Curtains still.
Is it temper that so stirs air?
Does air move of itself?
Or is it longing that rucks
the bedclothes
that lets the sigh go out?

A nurse says, ashes and urns and years later . . . *it's just
sometimes the newly-dead don't lie still, seem to live for a mo-
ment, move slightly, sigh or fart as a tiny pocket of air escapes.*

JACQUELINE BROWN

* from a sequence, 'Thinking Egg'

Finding

She channelled love under my skin
and left it there without a name.
I could not, would not speak of it.

Many nights there were ghosts about.
I held my breath, listened intent.
Questions came from under my skin.

Where was she? Not at the swings.
Not by the sea collecting shells.
I would not, could not speak of it.

Siren's wail banished ghosts to graves,
quickened I set out on a search
guided by cells under my skin.

Air was full of questions and names.
Hush–hush who came and went and where.
I could not, would not speak of it.

Years on the summer night is warm.
Moth–like, a touch releases love
trapped so long under my skin.
I dance and cry and speak of it.

CELIA BARRY

Searching

My mother lives here, I am told.
They give me her photograph,
a town's name, name of a station.

I begin at the beginning –
take a train slowly through an Oxfordshire autumn;
liquorice strip soil half-ploughed,
flat sheets of sky. One woman is in view –
her Alice-banded Nanny's face tipped open
like a palm, to beg the sun.

The single surprise of a gasometer,
giant barrel full of emptiness,
leads unremarkably to this:
a book-stand, coffee shop;
a platform, waited for,
to which I give myself,
lulled by track, by parallels.

Of course, there will be no one here.
Despite this search, no cobwebs
fanning corners, dusty recesses;

only faceless women
with their brooms and water,
sluicing stomach, cold as sky.

CATHY GRINDROD

On Shutting the Door

Often, when I leave home,
I think of you,
How you'd have shut the door
That last time
They fetched you out at dawn.

What fears would prophesy,
What intimations
Could foretell the terrors
Of those plains,
The herding into ash?

Or maybe, you looked round
As if before
A holiday, leaving
No trace of dust,
No crumbs for pests, no moths

In cupboards, carpets;
Covered the chairs,
The settee from the glare
Of light and sun,
Turned off the water, gas . . .

LOTTE KRAMER

Heading for the Heights

Why did she seek out the mountains –
January, force nines yelling,
the black bog, minimal tracks rained out,
the waterfall, iced solid?

Where all sane people were boarded up,
not daring to venture far from
their hot pipes, when her children called –
why need she go? What drove her?

The same, perhaps, that drives me from
the car-infested valleys,
to climb, till only the ancient pack-roads
are left, on top of the world.

You see them, heading for the heights,
on most mornings this winter,
equipped, you think, for the long haul –
maps, snow-boots and compass.

Wander all night. Doctors and missionaries
untraced, lone farms inaccessible;
how easy, on the calmest day,
to lose your track and perish.

Each year the bodies lie unclaimed,
and some, never discovered.
Yet still they head for the high ground,
no child's crying will stop them.

MERRYN WILLIAMS

from 'Poems of Memory'

The knife reduces a polished oval
to mimosa on the chopping board.
Free of the shell, day-old chicks tumble

like mimosa from their box onto the floor.
Animated egg — egg sacrificed!
My mother or myself scraping the board.

Only some forty years divide
these women. Time enough for her
to die. Almost my whole life

so far. And then, how much further?
How keen and clear these seventeenth-century
broodings make each everyday pleasure,

Everywoman's task. Her hands were ugly
with domestic scars, by which I remember them now
(mine are less scarred, less gentle) most exactly.

As if on a desert island, she knew how
to make do. A harp made with string
and nails, from a fire-log, somehow

tuned to all the songs I wanted to sing
in the secret, sacred willow above the nettles,
where she pretended not to know I was hiding.

Making do. Making sacred. The magic spells
love works on coincidence. I don't need
to be told what that letter tells —

unanswerable, a friend's fatal disease.
These chores tell it all in miniature.
And what is missing, memory supplies.

Folded, unanswered, a white blur
on the table-top, it becomes part of our home,
the sign of another marriage in our décor.

Signs in each other's lives, across time
also, though not always recognised, keep faith.
I know now that my mother used to climb

such a secret tree, pollarded, springing. Faith
with that memory helped her to let me hide
despite 'Lunch ready!' (and the rest). Near-death
of a friend is now what I think of, turned aside.

ANNE CLUYSENAAR

Mushrooms

She'd always peeled them;
slipping knife's edge under their lips,
pulling, tearing back the skins
in V-shaped strips to the crown,
turned them round in work-worn hands
which had washed and scrubbed us.

I hold their fruitful bodies,
smell each peat-dug stipe,
taste their tempers, pepper-hot
then stop. I think of peeling them
but looking down leave well alone
and pop them in a tempered pan.

She'd always polished them;
Brassoed doorknobs, fungal round,
buffing off our fingerprints
(she'd handled them like mushrooms)
and if she could I'm sure she would
have cooked them in garlic butter.

MOIRA CLARK

46

There

She's there in the way you mark a cross
with the point of a knife
on the bleak roots of the sprouts.
In the way you roll your thumbs in silence
through the long evening.

The boiler throbs in her warm kitchen
where the field mice scrabble at night
and the household dog quivers in dream.
She's there.
Her earth green apron levels the mounds of her body
and the swollen tea cosy waits on the table
in the place where you ate the gingerbread men
head first, better than the gradual nibbling at the limbs.

She's there in the way you walk
fixing your gaze to the grid of the pavement,
in the way your chin wobbles when you will not cry.

There in the garden where through the slats in the fence
you can just glimpse the shimmering girl in pink
the forbidden girl, whose mother keeps chickens,
whose father flings swear words into the slow afternoon.
She's there with you
knitting in the shade, watching you dig deep in the sandpit
deep enough to get right in.

In the chill in your stomach at the calling of your name
she's there. In the snarling of your thoughts
at the touch of skin soft words.

Behind the housefront crossed with painted beams
and the windows blocked with the backs of mirrors
she's there.
On the front door a red glass tulip lifts like a chalice
and down the hall where the carpet strains
between black stained boards
she's there.
And there's a long chain on the lavatory pull

47

and a heaving and a heart beat silence
before the wedding dress frothing of the water.

In the house where one icy afternoon
she brought in clothes from the line
rigid with frost.
Look! she laughed, showing her teeth. See!

How the trousers stood up on end
and the dress was hollow.

CAROLINE NATZLER

Changing

Crutch slipping towel over
bobbing white bottoms,
my mother said: 'Turn your back to the cave's mouth'.
Fighting wet one piece skin
over the thighs,
my mother said: 'Someone's coming'.
Caught on a toe, peeling the leg elastic through,
but bottoms are rude –
hide the flat chest, hairless groove?
My mother said: 'Take a large towel'.
Back in the damp, sucking, tide-line cave,
knickers on first, sticking,
towel trapped by vest, keep it down, keep it down.
My mother said: 'Something is showing'.
Button up. I'm decent I said.

Plunge in the pool, hair drifting, breasts drifting.
I'm fifty, I'm naked, I'm decent I said.

DAPHNE ROCK

Hair

A child my mother
braided my hair
in two tight plaits.

A teenager she coiled
about my head
plaits long as ropes

secured with hair-pins.
This style my classmates
called my crown of thorns.

Now middle-aged
a thistle
gone to seed

my white hair short
and free
to flirt with every breeze.

BREDA SULLIVAN

Exorcism

Under the harsh light, scolded by the Book,
in the flickering candlelight she is a snake,
a sow, ferret, sheep, bitch, cow, walrus, whale.

We have to hold her down. She cries out, *Mother!*
don't leave me!

       We should have known. Oh we did know
really. That sly look, the mouth drawn up,
the sharp teeth, the tongue shining with spittle,
the voice prissy as if reciting a lesson.

Oh no dear, that's not the way! Let me show you.
Still not quite right yet though is it?
Have you tried anything for those spots?
Never wear trousers with your thighs.
Don't you think black makes you look sallow?
Are you quite sure he's right for you?
You don't want to put it off too long.
Should she be crying like that? Should
she be walking by now? He's been out a lot
lately. Working hard is he? Oh.

She vomits it all up, black, viscous,
it distorts her mouth, slides down her chin,
grows legs and scuttles away like a great black rat.

She is limp now. She is speechless.
Of course she hasn't been herself
since she lost her mother.

DOROTHY NIMMO

Letter

That familiar curving hand.
Flat and white I unfold
my mother from a single
ruled sheet, shake out
the envelope in case
I've missed her.

Our letters pass like ghosts,
thin and pale they slip
through our mail boxes.
In my dreams she comes
sweet smelling, pinched waist
in a dirndl skirt, with lint
and Savlon to make poultices
for my grazed knee. Like Gretel
I try to track the pecked crumbs
to find my way home.

           I do not know
where to search for her. Deep
in her glass house she pricks
out seedlings, snaps yellow leaves
from last year's geraniums.

SUE HUBBARD

Libation

The next time my mother comes to visit
I will run her a bath
Perfumed with rose orange
And floating Gardenias,
Tenderly wash her body
The one which had housed
Nourished and held me . . .

After bathing
I tie a lapis blue cord around her waist
For protection
And in remembrance of our joining
Wrap her in rose pink cloth
And hold her tight
For all of her broken dreams.

My mother blesses me
And I forgive her
For the longing and for leaving me.
She still keeps my first curl
In a locket around her neck.

I anoint her head with oil and rosemary
And remember it was not always grey.
Together we walk to my room
Cleansed with juniper
Rock sage and lavender.

Her love for me
Flows into the room
And envelops me.

She lies on my bed
And I let her dream.
When my mother awakes we drink Melissa tea.

PALORINE WILLIAMS

Distances

I see my mother waving – her unfussed
smiling au revoir, alone on her verandah,
a small figure half-covered by shadow.

I hold her wave, see myself sharing it
eightfold, once for each of us – a wave
we have grown into

as she perfected it, voiced it over years
listening for the two who died,
losses she carried into her skin,
her children – the only trophies
she ever wanted.

Now I search her face
contained, real as light,
hear over her words sewn into
the wave, 'There are many kinds of love
and I have lived some of them.'

KATHERINE GALLAGHER

54

Remission

When we took my mother
from hospital the first time
we watched her the way later
I would watch my first child
to be sure she'd breathe.

She almost couldn't walk upstairs.
My father and I, new parents,
flanked her for the climb
one step by one step. My
bigboned mother, taller
by two inches than her man, my mother
with her long feet and wide hips
and spreading do-it-now hands,
swayed between us while we steadied
an elbow each and pretended not to and she
raged at us for helping her.

Maybe she knew and maybe she didn't,
the little chrysalises hadn't left but crawled down
into the lymphnodes, into all
the secret parts of her, biding their time.
She made herself eat, she made herself walk,
she clawed back from us the things mothers do.

And when she almost had them all,
as if my body
had learned something I hadn't,
the nerves in my right shoulder
began firing, all by themselves
like deranged telephone wires, then I blistered
nape to wrist
in tiny amber beads of pure burn.
I was trapped in my flat,
not able to wear even a shirt.
Not able to wrench round to the source of the pain.
Twice a day the ointment meant to ease
had me striding up and down blaspheming the ceiling.
Fuck, Christ, fuck.

My mother was in heaven.
She came to see me, I think it was the first time
she did drive again, breathless, a little shaky.
I watched her lift from their crinkled wraps
her glass jar of soap, pale green, breathing leeks,
bread she'd punched up and slapped down
and baked herself, salt cheese.
I watched her find the buckled pan,
light the gas and stir.
And I who at thirteen had given up
the cakes she loved to make for us, who for years
had picked around the edge
of her northern stews, breast of lamb
and carrots, potatoes oozing their fat,
I who would not learn to cook
anything she ever had cooked,
offered her my hunger like a gift.

I was 34 years old and she was 73 and quite soon
nothing would taste good to her
and what she did eat
would turn her straw-gold
as the most delicate tea,
but that day she fed me
like a new hatched bird,
sickly, the little wizened skeleton pushing up,
a cramped umbrella, under the
puckering unfeathered skin,
the yolk on it smeary, not dry.

KATHERINE FROST

from 'Entries on Light'

Knocking on the door
    you open, after every
absence – yours or mine –
    as our grounds and elevations
realign themselves, you
    on the step below me, one
or both of the kids above
    I'm struck again as you
face me, turn your back, stricken
    by how small you are.

Bird mother, busy woodland
    creature mother
beginning small and ending small
    I don't believe that it's only
a kernel blown to husk
    the great revolve and vanishing-
point of our figure of eight
    as you cross the kitchen, lower
the gas and we, entering
    let the small shock pass

that is the shock: for
    watching your anxious steps
vanishing deep down corridors
    to return with gifts, it's more
with a sense of vastness, height
    that I see you shrink;
of radiance, like your candle
    lit in the daytime, that I notice
how pale your hair and skin seem
    beside ours.

Dwindling, as hollows
    deepen, brighten and what is
nearest catches light
    in the circle you inhabit and I
inherit, knowing my reach is smaller
    much too small to lift

and shawl you in my arms, fading
you intensify, like candlelight
on scalloped lace, in the pink
the very fabric of our lives.

MIMI KHALVATI

Broken Necklace

Her memory fragmented like a necklace.
Beads rolled out of sight between the cracks.
On hands and knees I searched, dust-pan and brush
sweeping up my anxious mother's pearls.

We held them to the light to see their colours.
I tried to tie the strands with safety knots,
caught them on the page with felt-tip pen.
Names escaped the tip of her tongue, teasing.

She took them from me one by one, remembering
and read the words aloud, holding fast
the thread that lead her through uncertainties
to islands in the past, where what remained

was incandescent . . . and lost the page until
I came again, knowing it by heart,
her golden chain that had no safety catch.

JILL BAMBER

Bathing My Mother

You hang back, call me
cruel, assure me you'll fall,
promise impossible behaviour,
anything to avoid that one step
into the treachery of white.

Years ago my baby daughter
would list implausible excuses –
a wobbly tooth, a hurting finger,
because her teddy said so –
to escape the ordeal of water.

Once in, of course, you're soothed,
though you won't admit it, fiddle
with bubbles while I soap your skin –
so thin, but soft as a child's –
fumble into intimacies,

glad of steamed-up glasses.
Wrapped in a warm towel, later,
you punish me with stiff
resistance, as I pat talc
into your shrunk hollows,

my belly tight, braced against
your slight weight, your need,
your terror, my fury, a longing
which takes my breath away
for another baby I'll never bear.

FRANCES WILSON

Christmas Present for My Mother

Yes the bottle comes wrapped in bladderwrack,
in coils of slinky seaweed
and I'll pack it in a small wicker basket.
When you open it
seasmells will ooze out into your sitting room.
Quick we must take the bottle
and pour a streak of emerald green renewing oil
into your hot bath and
hurry to help you,
your claw-like leg, slowly over the edge
and lower your stooping hesitant body
into the pungent greenish hot spring.
We'll hover as you sigh
and lie back and say 'wonderful'
and your confusion, your grief, your wandering
will be steamed away
and your back will slowly become strong
and your voice as it used to be.
You'll push up out of the water forcefully
and call for your towel.
You won't be young again but
your strength will come back.
There'll be a whiff of you
in that old photograph on the seafront,
dressed in cascading streamers
of seaweed, laughing.

SUE MACINTYRE

The Naming of Flowers

(for my mother)

I wish I knew the names of flowers.
I used to ask you, not caring for the answers
but for your joy in knowing them,
when to plant, prune, feed.
Then, as the blossom, flowering in your eye,
failed to make the journey to your lips
I stopped asking, knowing you would rake your thoughts
fretting for lost petals.
Now, I leaf through your books, searching
for names with which to show you
your last garden.

JENNIE OSBORNE

I'll See You Down the Lane

Clutching the ward's wall rail,
My mother's off to feed the bantams.
Where's the bucket? Do they need more grit?

'Come along, dear. Back to your chair.'
'I have to feed the bantams.'
They take her back and give her Ed the duck.

Ed's in bed, his cap on squint.
One wing is loose and dripping stuffing.
He has a knowing, cross-eyed look, often remarked on.

That night my mother has a fall,
Struggling out of bed
To go and shut the bantams up.

She breaks her thigh bone. Now she cannot
Walk, but moves her arms and other leg
Frondily, like something under water.

She worries: is the black hen laying out?
I tell her I will sort the bantams
And bring a needle in to sew up Ed.

'I'll see you down the lane,' my mother says.

In the day room someone's crying
While she rocks a shabby tiger.
Caged in a corner, the parrot lady squawks.

ALISON PRYDE

Minding You

You say you want to go home.
Shall I drive you there, one last time?
Across the water,
over the Bog of Allen
and the great Shannon divide –
home, to Ballinahistle?
To the field that has been in your head
from seventeen years old
to seventy seven,
the years you have been away?

This is the in-field, just over
the parkeen wall, and past
the ancient stand-alone thorn
and the line of damson trees
Young Tony, your brother's son,
will show us again
the mounds and eskers of stones
he and his nephews have picked
like hard grey potatoes
from the field's ploughed lines.
Is it never done with,
the stone-picking in this field?

Seventy years ago,
your first grown-up work:
October potato-picking,
then the second
months-long harvest of stones
as winter's rain revealed them,
crop after crop.

I would take you now
and put cold stones in your hands
at the in-field's sodden edge,
lead you into December's
sticky furrows,
if touch, and step
could somehow bring you home,
here, in England,
to your own lost mind.

CATHERINE BYRON

Christmas Fare

The caviar of death between bread,
that's what we eat this Christmas –
black salt:
that's what you spit,
what you pass,
what you eat raw,
what you become,
what we lay between bread and eat;
it is our fare, our diet,
how we must be between slices of life,
between ramming breadcrumbs in birds,
heating the oven for Christmas Dinner.

'Not by bread alone' –
black salt in your look
when I wake you with fatuous words,
'It's Christmas, Mother'.

Your concentration,
your tar
between the sheets,
hidden.

Linen folds its thick wink
over the slow black underground stream
that flows through,
marks your flesh purple where it touches,
like salt thawing ice.

We say that you upstairs
are with us downstairs in spirit
as we eat meat and gravy,
duchesse potatoes, broccoli,
baby sprouts, carrots,
Christmas Pudding,
mince pie,
double cream.

DILYS WOOD

Alice's Cat, New Year's Eve 1990

It began well didn't it, all that euphoria
in Europe, but in the spring an old woman died.
Now a cat dwindles with the year,
an unnamed monster gnawing inside.

Pain is born with dignity in both cases.
The reek of faeces and urine
does not detract from this. Green eyes, luminous
with appeal, implore me to do what I can

which is not much. I change soiled bedding,
speak comforting words I do not believe,
wash, brush, fluff out and powder
in a futile effort to deceive

myself. Never one for much touching, now
she grasps my hands,
I was going to say,
as though her life depends

on it. One night I get into her bed.
She is restless. I try to calm
her. She holds me and talks of Dad.
I am bad-tempered, as I always seem

when woken in the middle of the night.
She understands. It is how I am.
When I touch my skeletal cat
he purrs though he can no longer stand

as if flesh will dematerialise
at the approach of death,
leaving only those green burning eyes,
like Alice's cat, to disappear on a breath.

ANNE GRIMES

End of the Row

All the way driving in
through the dark into which you'd fallen
I could only think of your hands
deft, sure, hemming my first gowns,
knitting bright jerseys, fitting, ordering
my life. 'You're mine,' you'd say,
telling me what to be. I disappointed you,
my hands grew big, wanted to hold reins,
love men, open books. Now your grasp
of family, fabric, time, had slipped,
misjudged the hold, the switch, and you
were in the dark.

The room you were to have guested
would go on waiting.
All you left behind was a small heap
of hard jewels and a piece of knitting,
a half-made evening gown.
Cast off too soon, too soon.

ANNE BORN

Fanfare

For Winifrid Fanthorpe, born 5th February 1895, died 13th November 1978.

You, in the old photographs, are always
The one with the melancholy half-smile, the one
Who couldn't quite relax into the joke.

My extrovert dog of a father,
With his ragtime blazer and his swimming togs
Tucked like a swiss roll under his arm,
Strides in his youth towards us down some esplanade,

Happy as Larry. You, on his other arm,
Are anxious about the weather forecast,
His overdraft, or early closing day.

You were good at predicting failures: marriages
Turned out wrong because you said they would.
You knew the rotations of armistice and war,
Watched politicians' fates with gloomy approval.

All your life you lived in a minefield,
And were pleased, in a quiet way, when mines
Exploded. You never actually said
I told you so, but we could tell you meant it.

Crisis was your element. You kept your funny stories,
Your music-hall songs for doodlebug and blitz-nights.
In the next cubicle, after a car-crash, I heard you
Amusing the nurses with your trench wit through the blood.

Magic alerted you. Green, knives and ladders
Will always scare me through your tabus.
Your nightmare was Christmas; so much organised
Compulsory whoopee to be got through.

You always had some stratagem for making
Happiness keep its distance. Disaster
Was what you planned for. You always
Had hoarded loaves or candles up your sleeve.

Houses crumbled around your ears, taps leaked,
Electric light bulbs went out all over England,
Because for you homes were only provisional,
Bivouacs on the stony mountain of living.

You were best at friendship with chars, gipsies,
Or very far-off foreigners. Well-meaning neighbours
Were dangerous because they lived near.

Me too you managed best at a distance. On the landline
From your dugout to mine, your nightly
Pass, friend was really often quite jovial.

You were the lonely figure in the doorway
Waving goodbye in the cold, going back to a sink-full
Of crockery dirtied by those you loved. We
Left you behind to deal with our crusts and gristle.

I know why you chose now to die. You foresaw
Us approaching the Delectable Mountains,
And didn't feel up to all the cheers and mafficking.

But how, dearest, will even you retain your
Special brand of hard-bitten stoicism
Among the halleluyas of the triumphant dead?

U. A. FANTHORPE

Left Rites

When mum, who never quit the Party,
died, the Red Army turned up,
her co-op Bentley, English as boot black,
trailing limos, slowed through Norwood Cemetery
where Mrs Beeton's bones are stocked
and Gothic piety has run to fruit.

They stood – peaks, epaulettes, a host
of scarlet stars, flanked by cherubs,
epitaphs, cracked angels. Rolling down
the limo glass, I winked. A cossack,
shamefaced, flushing, dived
behind the BBC pantechnicon.

By the chapel Zils purred. Inside, a comrade
spoke, her casket slid, her anthem rang:
and the last fight . . . The verger, not one of us,
switched off the tape too soon, before
The Internationale unites
the human race, but sure as the sky

dawned rosy over Dulwich, equal
among Old Bolsheviks, she watched – lights,
rolling, take thirteen – the Beeb shoot *Stalin*,
and chortled home with us to bourgeois tea;
then, tossing down vodka, clenching our fists,
we drank to Trotsky, Marx, mother's jokes.

HYLDA SIMS

Sorting Things Out

A wooden spoon.
A sieve. That special saucepan for the rice.
A toothpick–holder made of glass
(it travelled with us from Milan).
A bunch of porcelain flowers in fashion then.

Your father's letters
in that odd Ladino/Hebrew mix
(Ladino sound with Hebrew script).
Your brother's, when his wartime marriage failed;
the paper blotchy, dampened, then dried up.

Your clothes: the suit you did your teaching in;
the 'White House' blouses I'd bring from London;
the silver fox whose muzzle bit its tail-end with a grin.
The moiré dress and jacket, bluey-grey,
the seamstress made you for my wedding-day.

I haven't kept all these.
I've given them away.
I'm tired of keepsakes.

Your voice I'm keeping though,
your ringing Gallic voice close to my ear;
the rough feel of your hand scrubbing my back
the thick ring on your finger hurting me.

WANDA BARFORD

Migraine *

Here it comes again: vision bevel-edged
with rainbows, stuff dissolving even as I look
to liquid light, the firm world swimming
just beyond the rim of things.

There's a remedy today: the *migraleve*
they gave me from her medicine cupboard,
I being the daughter who'd inherited this,
and her skin, and the early grey in our hair.

It's the last thing I should be doing,
squinting at a screen at the still centre,
getting the words down before the onset
of vertigo and steel drums.

Then all I'll want is the green curtains drawn
in her room in the afternoon, sun-arrows splintering
her dressing table to a clutter of brushes and combs,
dustings of powder, its lipsticks and eau de cologne.

And her duck-down pillows and old-rose eiderdown,
her hand weightless and cool on my brow,
changing the scalding flannel for the cold one.
'A sick headache', they called it, when I was an infant.

She taught me to lie so still, the pain wouldn't find me.
If I drifted to sleep, she would creep away,
lifting her cool hand
too lightly to wake me.

GILLIAN CLARKE

* from a sequence, 'Glass'

I Do Not Want the Ceiling of the Sistine Chapel

I hated you; I confess I hated you,
for tossing away your talent, after art school,
for marrying, settling down and having me.
I watched you live your life vicariously,
and dissipate that gift on the family.

Once, as you stirred a vat of marmalade,
I challenged you and you shrugged and said:
'Obviously I didn't have the drive . . .'
But pestered by my own poor demons,
I – your child – refused to understand.

Now you're gone I look everywhere for traces
of your being – in places that you loved,
old letters, my own reflected face; I ransack
the stash of memories, finding nothing.
And almost giving up, I turn to your art.

The student oils depress me – that grimey portrait
of my bearded, glum great-grandfather,
whose canvas someone put a finger through,
the stiff flowers that hung in the Royal Academy . . .
but then I come across the sketch-books.

You never went on holiday without your paints.
I remember you, perching on rocks, in the sun . . .
I hear the tinkle of your brush in the water jar,
watch you lick the sable point and as it darts
across your knees, I fret again to see the picture.

Suddenly I understand. There's joy and life here –
in the white shelved bay with a placid sea,
the terracotta bowl of oranges and lemons,
the gaggle of beach umbrellas, that yucca
bursting into flower beneath a southern sky –

and my grievance crumbles like that ochre dust
on the snaking goat track up the mountains.
Great art – all that struggle and pain – may lie
elsewhere; who cares, for now I have my mother back.
I do not want the ceiling of the Sistine Chapel.

FELICITY NAPIER

Mother's Room

Right to the end you never got it straight,
the sturdy furniture that knocked
the corners off my childhood. Surfaces powdered
white like the evidence of your slapdash pastry,
drawers never closed and contents on the boil.
Clothes everywhere, the fur, the one good suit
jostling the crêpe and whalebone shabby tackle
rigging your old carcase.

The chimney, stuffed against the draught, now and again
gave birth to a crumpled portion of *The Guardian*.
The mirror faced the wall and never saw
your quick blind dab at the mouth with lipstick
('Do I look all right?'), ramming your strange hats
over disordered hair – unnaturally blackened
product of your wardrobe pharmacy,
the single blow you struck against the years.

Curtains, like you, were always on the move
jangling their rings, tugged furiously
across the glass, in case the man next door
mowing his lawn, or the plumber looking at drains
might see more of yourself than you cared to publish.
Oh it was all storm, it was whirlwind!
Never a day to spare for putting your house
to rights, for sitting back.

Where are you now
with your lambswool socks and toffee wrappers,
your photos on the wall?
Somebody else's taste papers the marks you made
but cannot rub you out, your curtains
hanging silently like records never played,
but every ridge and channel loaded still
with the commotion of your being.

NICKY RICE

The Last Apple

For sentimental reasons
I saved the last apple
Until it began to soften.
It sat in the kitchen
Neatly wrapped
In its bright square of paper
Torn from a catalogue.

Unwrapped
It was wrinkled, waxy
Bruised about the calyx
But warm
A perfect analogue for you
And what you did each year.

I see your hands
Thick fingered, dappled
Larger versions of my own
Working with precision
Tearing and tucking
Tray on tray
Of Bramleys away
Against the longest winter
And the wettest spring.
A breath of autumn
In a quiet room.

It's almost blossom time again
But you're not here
To taste your labour's fruit.
The sauces and the puddings
We create
All somehow last too long
Without your appetite
Your zest for apples
In any shape or form.

CAROL COIFFAIT

Mother

In sleep I saw my mother scrubbing stairs
and flailing through cupboards. She had
knocked out partition walls and put up nets,
stripped paint to faded paper.
Windows wide all night
had let in rain and drenched the Turkey rugs.
She'd axed mahogany and stuck
toytown plastic pictures over scars.

Why did she come, and in that mood?
More than twenty years ago, her death.
If she had rung the bell I'd have welcomed her,
given another chance to put things right
but no, she must prowl in the night
as I must still
leave doors unlatched.

DAPHNE ROCK

When the Camel is Dust it Goes Through the Needle's Eye

This hot summer wind
is tiring my mother.
It tires her to watch it
buffeting the poppies.
Down they bow
in their fluttering kimonos,
a suppressed populace,
an unpredictable dictator.

The silver-haired reeds
are also supplicants.
Stripped of its petals,
clematis looks grey
on the wall. My mother,
who never came here,
suggests it's too hot
to cook supper.

Her tiredness gets everywhere
like blown topsoil,
teasing my eyes and tongue,
wrinkling my skin.
Summer after summer, silt
becomes landfill between us,
level and walkable,
level, eventually, and simple.

ANNE STEVENSON

FATHERS

At the South Pole

This book is my link with father,
Whom I never succeeded in meeting,
Though we looked at each other.
Generation photographs show our like eyes,
Clouded and wide – the same secretive head.

Through childhood he wore this book,
Passed down to me. I put it on.

Inside the dark-blue cover
Separately in our ship we have both served.
Mind into mind, the gloomy engravings
Quickened and sailed through auroras of lonely land
In the childish acceptance. Inherited under a seal
That never broke, between father and me,
Into mature smile or the laughter of friends.

We feel our tall, our grinding tall ship's arc
Sharply raking beneath the Cross. The cabin boy's clingings
Loosen and fall. The cruel captain stands,
Eternal blackness and crack ice in his least word,
Pointless endurance. Of coming madness shriek the Horn winds.

Now the wrecked crew hones over wastes,
Roped on each other, dragging attempted salvagings
Beating for shelter. Intrepid mate
Saves little cabin boy from mesmeric clefts
Opening. Closing. Opening. Under engraved sleets.

Father and I have watched the albatross
Trusting the thermals. He turns his beak.
Above the glowing turquoise core of the berg,
Together we see the feathers of his neck.

JEAN EARLE

Saturday with Dad

Balding, already quite round,
Dad was zipped into fraying fawn cardigan,
baggy trousers. He sorted tools for
the allotment, tended greenhouse
plants, tucking in new cuttings,
weighing fat tomatoes in his hands.

Finding him, I took deep warm air gulps,
longed to grow roots, stay there forever,
be fed and watered in his glass cottage
of light where dirt was allowed and soft leaves
stroked my hot face wherever I turned.
He handed me hectic seed packets,

took his spade and basket of trowels.
I skipped beside him, hands in pockets,
reading seed language through paper –
hard grains waiting for his touch.
He let me make furrows for them to sleep in,
they needed his blessing to grow.

He boiled a tin kettle to make tea,
took a canvas stool from the tilting shed.
I arranged cotton on fruit bushes,
became a wild dancing scarecrow.
He scratched easily on thorns, bled a lot.
'I've got a thin skin,' he'd say, half smiling.

LIZ HOUGHTON

Stilt-walker

Knowing I would never be
tall enough, my father made me
stilts, two poles to shudder
and part under me
as I swayed among branches:
my back to the wall, I practised
mounting lightly, swung into air
between cherry-blossom, fascia-boards,
fanlights; I would totter
to the corner, stick-legged,
tap out my wooden circle,
one of those clowns who
thumb their noses at gravity,
their faces shrinking into distance,
long thighs arched over small
vehicles, the bulges of ordinary feet
swaddled in cloth,
striped trousers cut for giants,
or bell-tents of skirt so wide
they might conceal fat purses
of warm rubies, a baby's wet head,
a real man crouching.

SUSAN WICKS

Winners

Maps, his father said, are history –
told by the winners: you are where we say you are.
He'd learned that early. In '45, ahead of the Russians (just),
he left his pocket meadows and walked west.
Dodging armies he lost to the road
two sets of grandparents and a Swiss army knife
(Victorinox). He was fourteen.

In Berlin who noticed a boy? It was his for days
a city unpicked like a jigsaw by a bioscope god.
Later he moved to Hamburg, made good. Lucky
for some. Stalin razed the village
where his father's father was born – chasing
it seemed an American dream – it's
that old Midas-touch, peasants for wheat.

The Wall went up, came down. A whim one August –
they drove east. To a plain wiped clean as the map, the Volvo
a harvest-beetle nosing gold.
To trace what? The son thought of seance
and childhood scars you find – believe you find –
knowing they're there. No farm, tree, fence.
The bald claims of compass and wish.

Once, a breakthrough of green, and once a watermark
on the silk surface wondered 'House?'
His father was not a man to cry. And indeed there was nothing
in the world to cry for. He stood and watched him lean
sideways on the levelling wind –
his cheeks washed by the blown-back glitter
of corn racing itself from sky to sky.

KATHERINE FROST

Spanish Peasant Boy *

after a drawing by Benjamín Palencia

Perhaps you have sworn
to be still like this,
in your loud stone boots
your cropped hair
and sleeves too short
in a ploughed field,
the civil war
still far from your village.

You can hear it already
and pay attention.
It will come, one day,
right into the square
the sheep pass over
as my hand passes over
this paper, into the fastnesses
of doorways and sheepfolds.

Perhaps you will see my father
in the band of soldiers
with his hair cropped too,
the cypresses toiling
along the edge of your field.
Perhaps you will leave everything
as he did

and cross borders,
go to France, America,
anywhere that will have you.

JANE DURAN

* from a sequence, 'Silences from the Spanish Civil War'

The Pyrenees *

Today I met you, son of a Spanish exile
in a London café, far from Mexico
where you grew up, I far from my native New York.
We talked about our fathers.
Both died before Franco died.
Neither returned to Spain.

When you told me your father's story,
we were in that invisible cage
I imagine the children of exiles live in,
open to wind and night.
My eyes filled with tears

and the wires of the cage lit up for a moment
so all those photographs I had seen
became moving people, breathing,
heavy with rain, suitcases, blankets,
warm with their pasts still inside them

pressing against the wires of the cage
that war and our fathers made for us.
Enter, we said, Enter, welcome.

JANE DURAN

* from a sequence, 'Silences from the Spanish Civil War'

The Non-Emigrant

(my father in Nazi Germany)

He left his application forms
Hidden inside his desk and missed
His quota for the U.S.A.

He thought he'd stay and wait and stare
The madness out. It could not last.
He would not emigrate, not lose

His home, his language and his ground.
Beside his armchair sat a pile
Of books; the smoke from his cigar

Fenced comfort with a yellow screen.
His daily walk was all he'd need
He thought. Abroad was where he'd been.

LOTTE KRAMER

Bluetits

Thinking they'd fledged too soon
he carried the bluetits back
to their late-brood nest.
She remembered the ladder bending
and him scratching an ear
as they all came fluttering down again.

Before that, the garden had been hers.
She'd search for snails in the long wet grass
and lay them out in rows
shrinking their horns with her fingertips
or fly on the rickety swing
till her toes touched apple boughs.

All she'd known of him then
were the flimsy aerograms
he always wrote in careful capitals
about the geckos on his walls
and how he stamped
to scare away the snakes.

When he returned, she tried
to find a likeness in his photograph
but it wasn't there.
This man was fat and shiny
with a moustache that didn't match his hair.

He mended the swing though
and the snails curled up elsewhere
while he mowed the lawn
and made a parade ground
for the flowers.

Then the bluetits flew.
Watching the last of them
they stood together
laughing at his anxious parenting.

RUTH SMITH

Dürer's 'Young Hare'

This hare which scampers into age and death
conjures a smile across my father's face.
White blossom, spotless bunnies mark the page
with dappled currents in an Easter wood.

He was young, then, and strong, and called me
Child
amongst the damp and fragrant violets
stuck to his rucksack for my mother's jugs.
I thought a wicked witch had made him old.

His fishing friend had seen the bluebells twitch
and copses torn around a lucid dell
crawling with rabbits crazed in agony:
myxomatosis, miles from vets and 'phones.

They had no guns: fetched rocks to smash the skulls.
I close the book I brought and watch him grope
through opening buds to vomit in the stream
and feel with hazel wands for naked springs
I can't pull out of hatted Evensong.

NORAH HILL

Forest

For my father

Yes, you must have had the camera
With its cracked leather strap
And celluloid red disc,
But I will remember you
By the fullest moon
Over the lowest tide on Sutton Sands.

Just the two of us.
Our thirtyish years between
Far out at sea that night.
I was seven, seventeen and seventy.
You said to wait and watch,
Listen for that last wave's slap
Before the turn. *Ssh. Soon!*

Meanwhile, the moon enjoyed the beach.
Scampering, it left silver footprints
Among the cockleshells
Along its flat length.
Soon!

And you stood rock-still,
Your eyes constant on the drawn-back
Sea. Waiting. Only your gabardine flapped,
Sound-tracked the mystery.
Then I knew I didn't want *soon* to begin.
I didn't want our waiting to stop.

The glittering black stumps
Emerge from their underwater clay-beds
Slowly.
Rank after stoic rank horizon.
Fossils glisten in their fissures.
All history now.

PRISCILLA BORTHWICK

Anyway,

I think it happened –
that I went down with him
to greet the day, skinny-legged
in the morning sun,
down to the seafront stalls
where you get drunk
on seagull-screeching smells,
where cockles and mussels
sunbathe in white saucers and
the raw breeze scours your lungs.
Me and Dad. And
the ridged sands were
glittering corduroy.
They smiled
as if they might believe me.

It was a different summer
when we had strawberries for tea
from the bowl with three glass feet
that came out for the Christmas
sherry trifle and I stammered
we must keep some for Dad, he'd
be coming soon.
Freezing white
in their eyes told me. My turn
to believe them.

I dropped the dish today. One
glass foot sits now on the shelf. One
strong day I'll let my glass feet go.

BARBARA JAGGER

93

Little Red Riding Hood and the Wolf

I hold up my chin
as Mum fastens the buttons
and ties up the hood of my red shiny mac.

'Tell Granny we love her
and give her these cakes and these flowers.
But beware in the woods.'

Red is the light of the day on my head
through my crimson umbrella:
a shield from the footsteps of rain.

Daddy holds out his hand
and I take it – the path is all
slippy and sloshy with wet.

The quicksilver bole of the beech
is the pole of a tent and the pattern of leaves
on the grey of the sky is a roof.

I am cold, my legs bare. But I do as I'm told
in the wet and the rustle
and the grunt of the whispers of the wood.

Granny caresses my cheek and my hair:
'You look pale dear; your lip trembles
and, oh your hand shakes.

The wind in the trees should bring
roses of joy to your skin,
when you walk with your daddy,

You're safe with your daddy,
he's so big and so strong with such a sharp axe,
and he loves you so much.'

GILLIE BOLTON

Crab

As my shadow touches them
crabs scuttle like the severed hand
in Maupassant's story, returning me
to unlit stairs, wallpaper faces
emerging from the dark.

It's tea time. A red-boiled crab lies
stricken on its back. My father
fuddled and morose, rattles through
the scullery drawers for skewers
and a hammer to crack the claws,

working the tender meat into pink,
poking around in the tangled heap,
slewed with drink, he fishes out
poisonous green feathery lungs:
dead man's fingers.

It's morning, the shaving mirror
all steamed up. My drowned face
watching him tussle off my white
school blouse, his eyes closed,
head thrown back, betrayed by sweat,
stroking my goosepimple breasts.

ANGELA DOVE

Laughing All the Way

Once late at night staying in Menton
I found my father outside the bedroom door
at the Hotel des Anglais
swapping the paired shoes along the corridor.
I couldn't sleep that night. What if
the bootboy challenged me?
Next day we walked the dusty road to Castellar.
At every garden door he rang the bell
a challenge to the villa-owning 'Chiens Mechants'
half hidden in the trail of bougainvillaea.
I wanted to run but he held my hand,
deliberately slowed his pace.
Back home he played on my fear of dogs
shouting from the top of Hampstead Heath
his voice echoing to St Paul's, the Surrey hills,
'Help, this dachshund's after me.'
He always sliced fruit cake horizontally
taking the topmost nut-packed slice;
made Mothers most-to-be-revered guests blush
with 'Would you fancy some of the tarts we're keeping for
tomorrow?'
And after every evening meal
informed my mother categorically
that for once he'd not be helping with the washing up.
She'd fallen for him when still at school,
he'd wooed her, urging his Great Dane,
'Go for her,' he'd said. She'd gone for him.
I was away at college when he died.
I wonder if he laughed to hear the final diagnosis
turn upset stomach into heart attack.

LIZ CASHDAN

Looking North

He was a South-of-Watford man.
Few places that lay North of that marker
gained his approval – though parts of Suffolk
were O.K., and he tolerated Wales, especially
the area around Llandrindod Wells.

As far as he was concerned Northampton,
Durham and Derby scarcely existed.
It's taken me a lifetime to revise his judgements –
to discover, for instance, that Manchester
is no wetter than Cornwall, and has theatres,

even a tree or two. Liverpool especially
came as a surprise, my having been brought up
to believe it a city in which no sensible person
would wish to set foot, let alone settle.
An aunt who went to live there

was spoken of almost as if dead.
He envisaged a pall of yellowish fog,
a population scarcely human – the dregs
of the world's most noisome seaports.
Of course he never went there

but I remember how his lip would curl
at the mere mention of Liverpool.

PAMELA GILLILAN

Fatherhood

I can't remember really envying them,
those girls, who lived, unpardonably,
exactly opposite our house.
Girls, whose puberty was a slow rounding,
a blossoming, whose
hair swung and shone, whose
skin, sweetly tanned, invited touch,
commanded it even.
Girls sought out for every social sport,
besieged on every dance floor,
their every contribution lauded
in golf club conversation.

But I can remember my father
envying their father;
still hear him say
'I'd like to buy that bunch,'
each time he saw the trio of golden girls.
'Just waiting to be *snapped up*,'
he'd go on to say,
believing his status in the club
rested less on his handicap at golf
than on that subtler handicap,
his chance of winning the unspoken race
to give one's girl away.

JOAN WADDLETON

My Father Makes a Lightbox
for Vivienne Westwood

I grew up with the language of electrics;
conduit, trunking boxes, spurs.
Amps – round in my mind, blue faced,
Voltage a wicked witch.
From his grimy bag of clips and fittings
I peopled schools, dramas, feuds across our floor.

Fully earthed – he saw his girls through puberty
like a reliable appliance, insulated, dozing
in the fabric of his shirt like the hard work smell
brought home from other people's basements, lofts.
I helped sometimes, big houses,
Holland Park, Cadogan Square –
listening for cable he'd feed to me through ceilings,
dialogue of taps, triumphant double tug.

Retired – he does the odd job now and then
like this lightbox he made the other week,
'Frumpy old tweed skirt she had on,' he told me
'Hair a mess.'
She'd offered him the freedom of her kitchen.
He'd have his flask and sandwich on her stairs.

NICOLETTE GOLDING

Phoenix

A thousand miles and two world wars
Separate our births. A rime
Of white hairs and nightmares his legacy;
Pigtails and nightingales mine.

I can hear something fluttering –
Fluttering like a child's heartbeat
In the sealed-off chimney
That once served a range.
'Do something, tatuś. Please.'
He nods. Fetches a hammer.
Wages war with a cold chisel,
Trapping debris in a curtain.
Iron hits the wall, each blow
A polished detonation of sound.
Bricks and mortar flake away
Like shell fragments, against
A telling background of silence.
'Felix . . .' My mother, shocked;
Appalled at such destruction.
Whoosh. A cascade of soot –
Feathers, stones, tiny bones;
Echoes. A black hole opens up.
We listen. And then . . . a coup.
A scratching, a scrabbling,
A shower of ashes. 'What now?'
'Ve vait,' he says.

A dove emerges, blinking,
Thin, bedraggled refugee.
My father opens the door –
And, smiling, sets it free.

ELIZABETH KAY

Tatuś – pronounced tatoosh; Polish for daddy.

My Father's Words

Perhaps it was the fishing boat
on the still glass of the water
that made me think of you

bursting to the surface off the coast
of Argentina. How often I'd
goad you into telling!

Suddenly, in your twenties,
speech deserted you; you searched
in vain through Liverpool

to track down its thief. When your teeth
fell out, you fled the country,
peeling your passage on a trawler –

mountains of potatoes (and who knows
what past traumas), arriving mute
and penniless to begin a career

on the *Buenos Aires Morning Herald*.
For two years language was your hands.
Then one momentous day, diving offshore

with friends, you propelled yourself up
towards light and, with ears ringing, shot
through toughened skins – singing!

Shouting whole dictionaries of pure
exuberant Spanish! And perhaps
it was foam that flashed-me-back

bringing you the orange plastic
bowl to help you – too scared
to face your image – shave in bed.

And the steely mirror of the sea
reflecting, like the photo I took
of you, ghostly at the bedroom

window, the fine transparent line
dividing worlds and lives,
bringing me again a picture

of your shrunken, yellow
frightened face, smiling,
at sea among the pillows.

LUCY HAMILTON

Throwing Out my Father's Dictionary

Words grow shoots in the bin
with the eggshells and rotting fruit.
It's years since the back fell off
to reveal paper edged with toffee-glue.
The preface is stained – a cloud rises
towards the use of the swung dash.

My father's signature is centre page,
arching letters underlined – I see him
rifling through his second language.

I retrieve it.
It smells of tarragon – my father's
dictionary, not quite finished with.

I have my own, weightier
with thousands of recent entries
arranged for me – like *chador*
and *sick building syndrome*
in the new wider pages.
I daren't inscribe my name.

MONIZA ALVI

My Father's Dreams

A brown berry of a man, bald head
burnished by days of gardening,
he spoke with his hands, gave each task
complete concentration, complete care.
People he avoided. I never knew
what his grey eyes saw.

Love was declared in a doll's house,
a circus ring, fitted out to
the smallest monkey. Later in golden
pie crusts, beef curled exact around
a nub of kidney. Twenty
Benson and Hedges left for me.

He didn't deal in words except
when visited by his rare dreams.
They unfurled with the complexity
of a Victorian novel, plot
enclosing plot, a narrative
that twisted down real streets,

conjured characters who spoke
through his quiet voice, mouth scarcely
moving, mysterious. I sat as
worlds crammed into minutes' sleep
unfolded in his words, a perfect plot
curled to its resolution.

'So that is what my father dreams,'
the wonder of it in my head all day,
walking back from school at night
through the unexpected places of his mind.

CYNTHIA FULLER

Earth Man

How can I speak your spirit
  in the small skin of a poem?
The drive in you, building your world
  stone by rough stone, a mountain.

Flint-eyed and wistful to equal degrees.
  Watching the world from an eyrie,
a distance I could not quite cross.
  The habit, not choice, of your generation.

Parenting behind *Fowler's Moon*,
  Palisades of rods or guns.
Stumbling through stories
  with an earthy voice: the slow-tongued

vowels of the fens; or wading
  across with shy hands
from a haze of grass-clippings,
  turps, plucked feathers,

black smuts of woodsmoke
  in simmers of air.
How can I speak your spirit
  when we perplexed each other?

You'd scan this page without seeing,
  hawk-eyes poised between hazel
and green, preferring bones
  to a paper skin. Earth man,

handling pheasants, roach,
  with barbaric tenderness.
Your palms red as rush-lights,
  the quiet welling through you

like sap. Overflowing
  your limestone face while
my mother's words fussed round
  like hens, cheerfully pecking

at your fence. Sunflowers peering
  round the deep blue cave
of your silence. Where words
  decalcified in ones or twos

aye, yes, the wind's up,
  as you hauled off your boots,
the weather scribed on your back
  in zig-zag mercury. It was

your way to walk in silence.
  Shoulder the wind, then stand
like a single thorn in a field.
  Inhaling the land, letting

its clay-with-flints uphold you,
  light on gulls' wings fill you.
Travelling in your eyes
  to the skyline of your spirit.

LYNNE WYCHERLEY

Cracking Walnuts

He cracked them in half
turning the shells
in his large hands
into small boats,
with match stick masts
and paper sails.
They floated bobbing up and down
in the sink or bath, sometimes capsized.
Perhaps he also told stories
about his father making boats
out of walnut shells for him.

After all this time, I still don't know
how to talk to him.
We speak about clutch cables
or compressor valves. He gives
good advice about plumbing
more rarely bad advice about love.
He tries to head me off,
to warn me against taking any risk,
he who followed Mama and us
across the Iron Curtain,
never to see his own father again.
His heavy hands on my shoulders,
push me out to sail away
and hold me back, both at once.

These days he forgets most
of what we say,
but not everything. When I visit
we sit round the same table
he still cracks walnuts open
passing me broken pieces to eat.
But sometimes he manages
to pull out a whole half
creamy coloured and perfectly formed
all crinkly and brand new.
Silently he hands me
a hard nut heart.

MARIA JASTRZĘBSKA

The Woman Who Mistook her Father for an Irishman

He was an upright man, a too-tight man
a man of honour, a man of blight, a sight
of land, a one-man band, a sweet tobacco
curling in the wool of his all-English coat.

He ruled, he puffed, he parked the car
in twenty jolts and shifts, he lifts the
load, adds up the profit, calculates the loss
and doesn't give a toss for her undoing.

Looking after, she remembers, meant a window-seat
a pleated curtain, knives of bone, a battle won
taut strings, an overview, the one who always knew
the globe's best shape, its politics, its scars.

But when they watched the old films flicker, he
and his daughter, from the old plush seats that creak
with laughter; when Chaplin's tickle inches up
the legs and hits the belly hard and rattles there

and when they buckle into raucous groans
her father toppling headlong from his chair
is no more English than this lilt, this flare
of fiery sound that whips the heart to bits.

Then he's a tramp, a man whose song assaults
the Irish sea with unrequited love, until
the old gods tell him who he is and she can
recognise a rakish eye, a fiddler buried deep

and so far down her father's Irish heart is cleft
and hidden in his tweed, his socks, his tread
the rumbling of his wanton dreams in bed
air's hiss as he draws a breath of music

through his pipe, in the mean time of the year,
the catch of breath flaring his pipe's bowl
like a crucible, nations welded in the ash
his daughter's heart a carbon copy of his own.

NICKI JACKOWSKA

My Dada

Arguing liberation theology
with my Dada, who still prefers the divine
forefinger of the wholly furious Papa –
there comes a warm loud whumph over and above
the sunwarmed serpentine brick wall, and the white-
breasted cat loitering among the lilies
flees, one paw suspended first on the moss –
And again a higher, departing whumph – I
cry, Dada, look up, and there in the sky, flies
higher and higher a circus in the blue air:
red, blue and marigold yellow, a Big Top –
a balloon, rising with stately soft starts
of ignited gas, the fire at the top of heaven,
the Holy Fire on our blessed brows,
danced by the southwest wind across
the peach and the plum trees, and kept lit by
three Victorian gentlemen, whose faint black
top-hats grow hazier and higher. *Ora pro*
nobis, they begin to call down in Latin
but when last heard they're shouting: *Viva, Viva,*
Compañeros, Viva! and *No Paseran!*
And down between rose and lily, nervous cat
and wall, there come twirling three hats in one style,
three white sombreros. One my Dada wears now
and one I wear and one the small cat dreams in,
her nose alternately twitching with her tail.

JUDITH KAZANTZIS

The Therapist's Comment

'It's your father.'
'My father?'
'He's in you
like a sandbag.'

I smile,
shake my head.
My father needs protecting.
He gives blood,
has swollen legs,

prefers me
to hold a saw
so the teeth
won't jag.

Late at night
his washed spoons
hit the draining board
with a righteous click,
convex side up to drain.

If I dare to turn them
my face shows
upside-down
in the bent metal.

JENNY HAMLETT

Bo Tree

My father always wanted me to draw roses.
Could not understand my liking
for dustbins, craggy faces, demolition sites.

Nature's fine.
I've got ten plant pots bursting with it –
even a garden of sorts, trampled
by cats and small kids.

He tidies up the borders for me,
edges the lawn, prunes bushes.

I used to dig spiritual types,
knew several instances of enlightenment
(usually involving roses
or the pale green undersides of trees)
but it never stopped them lying, cheating,
leaving me to fend for the kids alone.

My father lets his spirit tend itself,
sees to the things that need his help.

I would draw roses for him if I could.

PATRICIA POGSON

Caustic Soda

The week the first baby died
my father visited –
awkward and lost in the new house
with stains on the floor
that would not fade.

While I was crying in hospital
he was on his knees,
not praying – scrubbing
with caustic soda and wire wool –
heedless for hours
with no gloves on.

He hid his red and bleeding hands –
said he hadn't felt the pain.
I held them gently, scolding,
not needing to say
that I'd learnt how it feels
to love your child that way.

LIZ HOUGHTON

Connecting Light

(for my father)

They were talking on the telephone about a low, drawn out
light with blackness to it. He'd forgotten her. He'd been late.
An unexpected softening in his voice as he remembered finding
her walking through the rhododendrons that dark afternoon.

He'd been late for her forty years ago. Now a chance conversation
about that time of day in winter when daylight fades into darkness
reminded him of the young girl and for a moment he felt the light
darken and the woman he was talking to became his child again.

SUSAN MICHIE

Upturn

My father at the front window
on a drizzled July Sunday
following a speck of orange
snail's pace across the bay —
too small to be of any matter.

Never at his best on a Sunday
he would fidget from Mass to tea-time
jingling the change in the pocket
of a dark blue suit, adjusting
the radiogram to Athlone.

He'd check again on and off.
Only when it was lost
to sight beyond the headland
did he knock on a neighbour's door.
They had the boat out in minutes.

And found the men in time
gripping an upturned hull.
Their arms and hands were numb
and would be for weeks —
the papers said next day.

Sundays went on the same,
my father restless, jingling,
keeping a watch on the open sea.

ANNE-MARIE FYFE

Embrace of the Electric Eel

For thirty-five years, Father, you were a numb-fish,
I couldn't quite remember what it felt like

that last time you hugged me when I was eight,
just before you went away.

But when you summon me to your stagnant pool,
Dad, Papa, whatever I should call the creature

that you are, now you finally ask for my love –
do you think I've become strong as the horses

Humboldt forced into a stream
to test the voltage of Amazonian eels?

writing later how he had never witnessed
'such a picturesque spectacle of nature'

as those great eels clamped against the bellies
of his threshing horses, how their eyes

almost popped out and their manes stood on end.
Though the jolt alone did not kill them,

many were so stunned they drowned.
That's how it is, Father, when you open your arms

and press your entire length against my trunk.

PASCALE PETIT

Erdywurble

My father's parents sold fish.
At school, Greek scholars taunted him,
the scholarship boy,
called him 'bromos', said he stank of fish.
His gifts withered; he learned
a stammer that stayed with him for life,
words jumping like the tiddlers he tried to catch
in the canal.

But from the fractured syllables, there grew
words of his own: 'Don't arrap',
he'd say when we were plaguing him.
'Pass me the erdywurble' – we in giggles
guessing what it was. 'I'm mogadored'
when the last crossword clue eluded him.
'It won't ackle', trying to splint
a broken geranium.

Unable to persuade the doctor
to help him die while he still knew himself,
his words trickled, stopped. Keening continually,
he stumbled on, mistaking night for day,
my mother for his own,
then recognizing no one. Just once,
answering his new granddaughter's cry, he said
'poor kippet'.

CAROLE SATYAMURTI

The Spoon Maker's Daughter

My head's too full of memories for my own good:
my father as a young man with blunt finger ends
his forehead then as smooth as the back of a spoon,
a shaper, a burnisher, a polisher of silver,
alchemical, a turner of dull metal into spoons.

A dozen for a baptism, apostle faced and fine,
vine leaves for a wedding set, the tracery of
families, arms for the nobility, rank by serried
rank of them laid out on green baize cloth.
His hands had their measure, those blunt finger ends

perfected balances of shaft and bowl, of shoulders
engineered to last — *a lifetime thing, a spoon* —
he'd say, and show me how to see myself reflected
upside down; my father as an old man with a blunt finger
ends and a head too full of memories to remember.

SUSAN UTTING

118

Ithaca-Liverpool

My father came today: an awaited visit,
the walk beachwards. Unusually quiet, he paced
the sand near the tide's persistent reach,
looking to the horizon broken by one dark ship.
'Like North Africa,' he said suddenly. 'The war.
Thought I'd never return. I used to watch
from the shore, as from a desert island,
the convoys passing endlessly
carrying soldiers to who knows what.'
His eyes held the distance; in their deep grey
was a lost boy, an Odysseus never getting home.
When the war ended, his plane approaching
English cliffs turned back, defeated by fog;
like a great gull banking, it landed at Paris –
a city he never asked to know. Even now,
haunted in dreams, he sees them,
the ghost ships passing silently, one by one.

GLADYS MARY COLES

Make Believe

Say I were not sixty,
say you weren't near-hundred,
say you were alive.
Say my verse was read
in some distant country,
and say you were idly turning the pages:

The blood washed from your shirt,
the tears from your eyes,
the earth from your bones;
neither missing since 1940,
nor dead as reported later
by a friend of a friend of a friend . . .

Quite dapper you stand in that bookshop
and chance upon my clues.

That is why at sixty
when some publisher asks me
for biographical details,
I still carefully give
the year of my birth,
the name of my hometown:

GERDA MAYER born '27, in Karlsbad,
Czechoslovakia . . . write to me, father.

GERDA MAYER

NOTE: The author's father, Arnold Stein, escaped from the
German concentration camp in Nisko in 1939, fled to
Russian-occupied Lemberg/Lwow, and then disappeared
in the summer of 1940. It is thought he may have died in
a Russian camp.

Meeting Place

You have left the train too early
I call out 'It's the wrong stop.'
See your jacket flapping, arms raised
as if to say goodbye.

Couldn't you see through the open window
that this place is not where we spoke about?

Your luggage sits under my feet,
an old fashioned square-edged suitcase,
'just one' you said, 'that's enough.'

We were sitting chatting of ordinary things,
when you jumped up and hurried off, perhaps
you thought this quiet station was your Adlestrop.

All I see now is a match-stick man, and I'm
shouting at it 'catch the next train, I'll wait
at the next stop.'

Now, fed up with waiting
I leave our luggage in 'lost property'
and hack-back, dangerously,
along the railway track.

Can almost hear blackbirds pecking at the sun.
Around the next corner I should see the station
a quiet place, and you sitting on a bench
admiring willow-herb and rosebay.

And inside my sprawling brain
I know this too is my Adlestrop.

PAULINE HAWKESWORTH

Night Fishing

From a distance – twilight's distance, which is measureless –
they stand identically bulked out, coat on coat,
stubborn-stumped as breakwaters watching the sea
creep fawning to their feet, retreat again. And he is there

among them, indistinguishable from the rest;
                                        no-one would guess
how frail, how warped his frame is now, how inside
the woollen gloves red blooms on his knuckles, veins
surface from the netting of each hand. He has escaped me,

joined this camaraderie of men who come to test
the dark, each bivouacked beside a tilted half-shell
sheltering a flask, a stool, spread ammunition:
weights spiked round like spurs, the crawling bait; trawling

from this long unfeatured beach for the treasures, wrecks
of childhood. Night will hang a curtain over what he does,
the night which rolls in with the tide and lights
a hundred lanterns springing white along the coast,
                                        unblinking,

inventing the lie of some vast road; along its route, as far
and further than the eye can see, they loom, rods straining,
lines stretched taut into the opaque hopefulness
of space. Distant sandbanks, shifting, tempt them:
                                        We are here,

they whisper, rising to be picked out palely by the moon,
altering the water's weave; this is where
the fish lie, softly waving their tails from side to side . . .
My father threads his hooks, adjusts the pendulum, leans back,

and casts. His shoulders, knees, crack out a warning
                                        in my ears –
he is so brittle beneath his camouflage of clothes –
I wait for it to happen, the overanxious throw
which sends him clattering down, rod leaping
                                        from his hands, his face

fish-white and small, bleached in his own lamp's light,
                                and no-one there
to see; and I am flying, struggling to return him
to familiarity, to drag him back
with me into any of the windblown weekend afternoons

of all the years we scoured the emptied beach together,
                                my hand
in his and warmer and more real than any lure
the sea tossed at our feet – which we threw back,
                                laughing:
snares of tangled line, the silvered cold of a lost weight.

CAROLINE PRICE

Cockatoo

After you've shown me the bedraggled cockatoo
you found in the wood-pile,
the cat-flap you've put in for the dog
she left you with,
you remember to put on the bright new shirt
you've held in your hand
since I arrived early, before you were quite ready,
remember to offer me tea.

I fetch out the shop-bought cake I brought
and listen to you talk,
wondering why you moved the clock
a foot along from the clean circle where it hung
all those years.
At a quarter past two, we hear the band in the street,
catch the tail-end of walking day
over the neighbours' fresh-cut hedges.

Where was I, you say,
going back to your tale of the Manchester cotton slaves,
the wakes week wagonettes, Poor Dick's
where men lay two abed – *not queers you understand,
they'd all have had a different woman each
in the pub yard* – where your step-father lodged
and learned his trade from the brickies
who talked themselves to sleep.

By the end of the afternoon,
we've got through the general strike,
bomb damage in Plymouth, and the way
Grandma Tinsley did her hair in coils around her ears.
I walk to the window, see you've let go the garden.
You are feeding the cockatoo on grass gone to seed.
Don't forget to tell your mother I've got a new bird,
you quip as I leave.

PAM BRIDGEMAN

My Father's Clothes

During the last nights of my father's life
I took refuge in his wardrobe

in the silence of its forest, among clothes
I had never seen him wear,

that he had not worn for years.
Silk shirts so light on their hangers

like the ghosts of tree people,
moonbeam blue and mist green

– all his pristine mornings
waiting for me to breathe on them

and perform my curing ceremony.
Suits of shining black and midnight blue,

fabrics I had to feel, summoning
his memories from their fibres,

expecting thorns to scratch my skin,
as if they required my blood.

Coats taking root in the wardrobe floor
like buttresses of great ceibas,

requesting me to crouch inside
their hollowed hearts, go with him

on his last walk.
Coats that had drunk his sweat

as he struggled up his apartment steps
dragging his portable oxygen,

that year when he could still
taste rain-feathers on his tongue,

his lungs squeezed to their roots,
the coats loosening their grip

as he grew thinner.
All my life I'd yearned

to press my face into these clothes,
had imagined a row of costumes

for him to disappear in:
a raven feather cloak or condorskin robe

– and to reappear in:
a bark cape or snow owl waistcoat.

And there, between the buttresses –
the last pair of shoes he wore

nestling together like sleeping deer
traces of mud on their hides.

PASCALE PETIT

A time of cherries

In the Valley of the Jerte
we watched the procession
of the cherry-pickers
under the eye of the black Christ.

I craved for pectin,
for the flesh of the *picota*,
and the noon-day siesta
under the shadowing trees.

Those things were rituals:
the pause at the Crucifix,
the basket of cherries
in their ruby-reds.

They were like life;
the sweet *picota*,
the bitter *morello*.
The flesh and the stone.

Barely a year later
we picked the crop
from our lone *morello*
under a grey sky.

You had blood-juice
on your hands
and your body was slow
with resignation,

as you moved
towards the absence of winter;
emptying yourself
into that final task.

SUZANNE BURROWS

By Heart

Because we're running out of time
for you to talk and me to listen,
I want to get things straight –

to know which brood of Holly Blue
feeds on ivy, spring or summer,
and what distinguishes the Gatekeeper

from the Meadow Brown, at twenty feet.
To hear you talk of flight patterns
and favourite plants, how Wood Whites drift

like snowflakes in the sun,
and even where the Devil's Bit persists,
the Marsh Fritillary's now rare.

I want you to remind me what was special
about that Hairstreak with the W
scrawled in white across its underwing –

as if knowing cancelled absence
and a father could be hoarded
piecemeal with the facts –

and, just in case, I'm keeping count
of all the times we've watched
and waited and given names to things,

memorising what you say
about natural things growing subtler
the more they're magnified,

while the opposite is true for us;
and how we tried to stir up clouds of wings
by hurling branches at a summer oak

and only saw a glimpse of silver –
though we knew for sure a whole colony
was feeding there, high up on the honeydew.

RUTH SHARMAN

Papa

On most nights now
you wander through this house
looking for lost words.

That rocking chair on the landing –
where I was shushed and nourished,
and later rocked myself to the floor
in the split of a forehead –
you touch its smooth round back,
edging it forward
as if it could give you what
you cannot remember.

Your mother's piano stands waiting
for the few letters that remain
in your fingers. Chopin moves
your hands, their memory
opening for a single prelude.

Tonight, in a blink,
you forgot my name,
but you have not yet forgotten
that I am your daughter.

BARBARA MARSH

Deep

The talk is of boats, sea-legs.
You boast your grand-daughter's got your genes
keeps her balance and her breakfast
in a Force Ten.

Five days out of hospital
and fifty-five years sideways
to the ferry from Scrabster to Stromness
I can almost feel your boots
braced in the bow
as it rolls down, lurches over
levels with the puffins' clockwork wings,
then rears to the sky.

And I'm at a loss to fathom you, father,
never a day off with sickness,
tired beyond moving, beyond dressing,
your tight lawyer's mind
alive with the seabirds off Skara Brae.

PATRICIA POGSON

The Colour of the Old Man's Eyes

'La jeunesse – elle s'en va et revient.'

It had taken this to notice
the true colour
of the old man's eyes

death's swing doors swinging
gently in the high blue summer room
death laying down the winter
of its body in raincoat dun
the colour I'd thought his eyes were

but his eyes were young

stone of azure behind the summer
white of gently turning clouds
his eyes were blue
ultramarine in the white caves
of his face, the sea breathing
quietly far away

his eyes were blue
young boundless–future
blue.

JUDY GAHAGAN

131

Leavetaking

Doubtful, I chose a bronze chrysanthemum,
'Don't buy flowers for a man,' he says,
his eyes on cricket, sees Gooch make a run.

Hears his young wife's voice – she long decades dead.
He missed her wildness that he'd trodden on,
would swim in cold seas – that's why she lost our son.

'Call up the men!' he tells the waiting nurse,
slim and uniformed – she's the bugle boy.
'You see them now?
They're coming down.' He slumps back in his bed.

'Two pints at The George!' he says –
a cheery leave. Still he hears the Somme.

VERONICA ROSPIGLIOSI

My Father, Counting Sheep

He has been awake
for long enough, counting.
His life is thick, painful
seconds, squeezed from the glass.

Stretching his eyes behind
the sharp sun's lance
he waits
for the terrible medicine of dark.

He has his mother's eyes.
Often she rapped his head
with bony knuckles,
her fierce hazel glint
searching out sin like truffles.

She never cured him of looking,
silk in the rag bag,
silver in clouds.

Now, his rib cage winnowed
with scorching breath,
his big glove puppet hands
tell their own story
to the sheets.

Somewhere in the dry
fields of his brain
he is driving his last
ragged thoughts relentlessly,
over and over.

What gives him quiet?
Not me with my bolus
of love and drugs.
My mother, her voice
shrill with familiar strain,
whispers angrily tender,
'let GO!' He sighs.
His flocks line up soberly.
All the mild sheep
are folded through his eyes.

KATE FOLEY

Baba Mostafa

He circles slowly and the walls of the room,
this Maryland cocoon, swirl as though the years
were not years but faces and he, at eighty,
in his warm woolly robe, were the last slow waltz.

'Children,' he would say, '*truly* love me!
And I have always, always loved children.'
'It's true,' she'd say, coming through the arch.
'Sarajune, you love Baba Mostafa, don't you?
D'you love Baba Mostafa or Maman Gitty, hah?
Here, eat this.' 'For God's sake, woman,
do you want her to choke! Come, Sarajune, dance . . .
da-dum, da-dum, da-dum, da-da . . .'

He circles slowly, the child on his shoulder
nestled like a violin and the ruches of a smile
on the corners of his lips as though the babygro'
beneath his hand were glissades of satin.

'Wunderschön! Das ist wunderschön!' He lingers
on the umlaut he learned as a student on a scholarship
from Reza Shah and on the lips of a Fräulein
whose embouchure lives on in him, takes him back
through all those years, through marriages, children,
reversals of fortune, remembering how in wartime
foodstuffs left his home for hers – manna from Isfahan,
sweetmeats from Yazd, dried fruit from Azarbaijan.

He circles slowly, on paisley whorls
that once were cypress-trees bowing to the wind,
as though these 'perfect moslems' were reflections
of his coat-tails lifting on a breeze from the floor.

'I swear to God,' he blubbered, only days before
his laryngotomy, 'I was a good man. I never stole.
And if – and who can say? – you never had the father
my other children had, God knows it wasn't in my hands.'
'How is he?' they whispered in doorways as I buried
my butt-ends in beds of azaleas. Months later,
he writes: 'I can't eat *gut* and sleep *gut*.' He never could:
holding up *Der Spiegel*, in the small hours, to the lamp.

And now he circles, from room to room,
with a grandchild for company who step by step
outstrips him as he learns – re-learns – to talk . . .
da-dum, da-dum, da-dum, da-da . . .

MIMI KHALVATI

Coma

Mr Khalvati? Larger than life he was;
too large to die so they wired him up on a bed.
Small as a soul he is on the mountain ledge.

Lids gone thin as a babe's. If it's mist he sees
it's no mist he knows by name. *Can you hear me,*
Mr Khalvati? Larger than life he was

and the death he dies large as the hands that once
drowned mine and the salt of his laugh in the wave.
Small as a soul he is on the mountain ledge.

Can you squeeze my hand? (Ach! Where are the hands
I held in mine to pull me back to the baize?)
Mr Khalvati? Larger than life he was

with these outstretched hands that squeezing squeeze
thin air. Wired he is, tired he is and there,
small as a soul he is on the mountain ledge.

No nudging him out of the nest. No one to help him
fall or fly, there's no coming back to the baize.
Mr Khalvati? Larger than life he was.
Small as a soul he is on the mountain ledge.

MIMI KHALVATI

Contact

Ritual done, sterile as Pilate
the team of surgeons gathers,
cuts, excises, cleanses.

Bloodied gloves are binned.

Your hands, my father, are the lifeline
for liquids dripping in,
for pulsebeats measured out.

Practical hands; your gestures make
a mime of actions showing how they stripped
the pins that stitched your chest.
And I remember watching
your hands at plane and chisel,
your fingers threading my shoelaces.

And suddenly I do not know
how to hold your hand. A nurse
sits with me, her arm across my shoulders,
twines my fingers around yours
to catch their last warm moments.

Before I leave, pick up the life you gave me,
I wash my hands.

ALISON CHISHOLM

Vigil

Mammals cling so! It must come
from the breast, this never wanting to let go.
Off to the west, a wolf stands
over the snowy body of his mate. How long
does he wait? Until her spirit struggles free
and dissipates? Through how many cold moons
does a prisoner's mother lie awake and listen
for the crack of bones? As many
as the racking breaths in an upstairs bedroom,
where an old man clutches his sheet
with hands the colour of gardenias
until his daughter whispers, 'You can go.'

And the small red animal inside my chest
waits only for the sun to rise and set,
and rise and set again
often enough for its own grief to be done.

BLAIR GIBB

Dilemma

As he lay dead,
frost-blue eyes hooded,
he looked like a Viking chieftain.
Grey-headed with strength and wisdom,
he needed no helmet or sword –
centuries slumbered in his folded arms.

They robed him in white;
and we were silent in his presence
listening for commands.
When fire had transformed
oakwood, roses, flesh, to ashes
we held the casket bewildered.
He had two wives;
and the dead wife was our mother;
but the widow cried, 'Scatter
them in the wood where he met me!'

Under the oaks, sowing, we paused,
dust on our hands:
'Let us divide him
as life divided him . . .'
So we emptied half on our mother's grave.
And no voice came from the yew tree
to question and condemn.

PHOEBE HESKETH

Father's Things

(i)

Items in an envelope. What he'd kept.

Snapshot. In a rowing club blazer and flannels,
Looking along his pipe at the wide, calm Trent.
       (A man I never knew.
       Young, handsome, happy)

Field Message, passed along the trenches. Please
Reinforce Hughes of C Coy with 14 Platoon.
Captain's pips. The usual medals.
       (Another stranger.
       Lonely, dogged, scared)

Dates. Birth. Left school. Left Lawrence's. Then
Self-employed. Retired. How long he worked, how old
At every stage; how many years the Army.
       (Known: not known.
       Wary, touchy, proud)

Accounts. Estimated annual expenditure. Suggested cuts
If necessary. No annual charges should be taken
Without careful consideration. Old age pension
Slightly increases income.
       (Known. Feared.
       Bitter, vengeful, blind)

Angry old man in a nursing home
       With a view of the sea.

(ii)

He bought me
A bedroom suite, which had
A semi-circular dressing-table
With drawers I discovered I could
Hide things behind.

He gave me
A bookcase, with all
The books that I asked for, and
Three years of growing up
Away from home.

He sent me one letter,
About being billetted at King's,
and about treacle.

He thought it all wasted,
As well he might.
I never said Thank you,
or Sorry.

R. V. BAILEY

I Have Taken the Suits and Shoes to Oxfam

I slide into his life,
glide into his geriatric ways.
I wind his wheezing grandfather clock,
I feed his birds and goldfish,
I sit for hours in his chair
and watch the fountain dribble.

I flush away his pills – the purple,
red and white – as I'm told to do.
I dispose of the two sets of teeth.
I dust and mop, though God knows why,
and find that fatal red cigar butt
underneath his bed, (they took the gun).

Yet there's no letter left for me
in his tiny, spider's writing,
no age-bruised hand extended
to a daughter, nothing to hang
my desolation on. But then
he knew that I'd know why.

I trim his patch of meadow grass,
yank bindweed from the border
and dredge up stalactites of slime
from his pond. Green entrails cling,
like memories, to the ramps of brick
he made for voles and hedgehogs.

I scrutinise the lists he made
on the backs of envelopes,
stare at the portrait of my mother,
feel the prick of his loneliness
and the cramp of his despair.
My world stops here.

FELICITY NAPIER

Smile for Daddy

At last he is quiet; his harsh words
can no longer scare the living daylights
out of me. I never understood the story
they told me of him in hospital asking
to see me, dressed in my new brown coat,
aged three or four. Today I wear my black.
Bartletts as far as the eye can see pack
the crematorium pews. Don't nick the books
of Common Prayer, the gilded lettering pleads.
He would have liked to see us all walking
in the rain behind a gun-carriage, his medals
lying on the polished coffin lid,
a sort of mini state funeral, the slow drums,
the tolling bells, the black veils.

He fought, but did not bleed or die
for his country, as he disciplined
but did not love his children.
Smile for Daddy. Somewhere there's a face
grimacing at a window, a small girl held high
in the air, a pale hand waving weakly.
All the men I've loved knock on wood,
and seem to wear his humourless stare,
used me for bayonet practice, went absent
without leave, could reduce me to tears,
as he did, but they were not aware
of this, and so we wait for him to disappear,
silenced at last, although not in my dreams,
but that is my funeral, not his.

ELIZABETH BARTLETT

Soup and Slavery

Yes, I can hear you, father,
at the other end of the line you invented
for us to phone on after you died.
I can hear your prolonged throat-clearing
like fork tines dragged over grit,
know you're preparing to speak.
I can even see the anger boiling up in your face
as I pull specked leaves from sprouts tighter
than fists, chop shining leeks into rings
for a soup I'm making to succour
the aged pair next door. Now you scald me:
Why are you making soup
for strangers when you wouldn't cook,
wouldn't take care of me?

I'm making soup
because it's not a duty that traps me
rabbit-helpless between metal teeth,
because it comforts me in winter
to smell the sizzle of softened onions,
because it doesn't occur to my old neighbour
to give in to shaky legs, shrinking body,
because he planed at his bench for years, grew
potatoes, gooseberries, sweet peas in his garden,
because he waits on his wife who's enjoyed
almost a century of delicate health,
because I've seen four pans steaming on his stove,
because love fuels his willing slavery,
because he'll call this soup *a godsend*.

All right, I knew you'd bark me down –
it wouldn't be you if you weren't top dog.
I can see you issuing instructions
up there as if you were still
in the Home, demanding special rights,
losing your temper with the cackhanded,
hounding the timid, passing judgement,
making up jokes for your favourites, offering
advice on finances, giving the thoughtful one

a cheque to buy panchromatic glasses –
oh I know your deep seam of kindness.

But I can't forget the jug.
Jug? you boom. Yes, the white-lipped jug
painted with roses, not even half full,
the jug you complained was a burden
to carry upstairs so that your dying wife
could totter to the kettle in her room, pour
your afternoon tea – she whose picture
you idolized after her death.
That jug is lodged inside me.

Jug! you bellow but I cut you off.
When I choose I can reconnect
to you at ninety-three, alert, probing
theories of the universe, explaining
the more we know the less we know;
or I can listen again to the story
of that sleepless night in 1943
when you struggled to solve in your head
the mystery of the gas the Germans
had packed into powerful missiles,
the eureka moment flooding
like the moon on a frosty lawn,
feel proud you helped shorten The War . . .

Yes, I can hear you father,
am sad I didn't cook you meals,
glad I'd slipped enough chains
to stay with myself. No need
to shout. Go back to bossing
the angels while I add a pinch of sage
and thyme to the barley-pearled soup.

MYRA SCHNEIDER

Dad

Your old hat hurts me, and those black
  fat raisins you liked to press into
my palm from your soft heavy hand.
  I see you staggering back up the path
with sacks of potatoes from some local farm,
  fresh eggs, flowers. Every day I grieve

for your great heart broken and you gone.
  You loved to watch the trees. This year
you did not see their Spring.
  The sky was freezing over the fen
as on that somewhere secretly appointed day
  you beached: cold, white-faced, shivering.

What happened, old bull, my loyal
  hoarse-voiced warrior? The hammer
blow that stopped you in your track
  and brought you to a hospital monitor
could not destroy your courage
  to the end you were
uncowed and unconcerned with pleasing anyone

I think of you now as once again safely
  at my mother's side, the earth as
chosen as a bed, and feel most sorrow for
  all that was gentle in
my childhood buried there
  already forfeit, now forever lost.

ELAINE FEINSTEIN

BOTH PARENTS

Before these Wars

In the early days of marriage
my parents go swimming in an empty sea,
cold as an echo, but somehow *theirs*,
for all its restless size.

From the year 1980 I watch them
putting on the foamy lace.
The sun's gold oils slide from their young skin
and hair, as they surface

to fling each other handfuls
of confetti – iced tinsel
and tissue, miniature horseshoes
of silver, white poppy petals.

I search their laughter in vain:
no baby twinkles there,
no Hitler marches on Poland
through the cornflower waves

this print shows pewter.
But that the impossible happens
eventually, everyone knows.
And when they swim away

the unsettled water fills
with shuddery, dismantled weddings,
a cloud unfurled like an oak-tree,
time twisting as it burns.

CAROL RUMENS

Letters from the Concertina File 1939–1940

Its lettered pleats and crevices
fit the privacy of marriage letters.
Deeper and deeper between you
I dive in, discovering among congratulations
and condolences domestic bonds – tightness
of her clothes after the latest baby –
her old Donegal skirt still fits.
Love and so much separation.
So much about us, about us –
the one whose face is like
an overripe plum, the troubles of another.
The sureness of climbing on the marriage platform,
the war eating it away, the swirling plans
changing each time you write,
fear petering out in desolation.

SUE MACINTYRE

My Mother Dressed for the Wedding

My mother dressed for the wedding
is a star: Astarté in a ballgown
bias-cut from the night sky, with a Milky Way
of sequins. She glitters, catches the light,
splits it into wine, sea, indigo.
Glossy her midnight hair, her silver sandals,
the carmine on her lips. She carries
her twelve stones proudly as a priestess.

Next day, her rounded arms are bare again.
Throned on a kitchen chair in backyard sunshine,
she holds the colander in a pinafore cradle
between splayed knees. Her capable hands
split pod after pod, thumb the peas down
to swell the galaxy. I crunch pods:
milk and jade on my tongue, prophesying
sweetness. Translucent shards remain.

My dad had been shelled too. Shrapnel
had split his skull, thumbed his brain.
'I've got a plate in my head,' he'd say.
I thought of bone china. Now she keeps
the world turning, plates on the table
regular as sunrise. She is tireless
though the heap of peas takes aeons to grow.
For this moment she holds eternity in her lap.

STEVIE KRAYER

The Hit Men

Pip's sister, Mrs Joe Gargery,
Who had black hair,
Licked Pip with Tickler,
A springy cane,
When she was on the rampage.
I was nicknamed Pippa
And thought Hitler
Wished to hit the British
Like Mummy hit me.
They had black hair, too,
And moustaches. Did Mrs Joe?

We beat the Bosch
But Mummy still beat me,
And Daddy flicked me
With his long, whippy, suede-covered
Whale-bone, shoe-horn:
I called it his Flipper.
After the War
Hazel's husband, Donald, came home
From a Jap P.O.W. camp.

The Nips had beaten Donald,
And made him do slave labour
(That's nasty work, unpaid)
Just like me.
But Mummy and Daddy said how inhuman,
Cruel, uncivilised, barbaric –
A breach of the Beaver Prevention.
The Japs were smaller than Donald,
Who was six foot five
And got an executive job through a friend.

PHILIPPA LAWRENCE

Either Way

. . . for the roses
Had the look of flowers that are looked at.
T.S. Eliot, 'Burnt Norton'

The front wheel's off the mountainside
the 40s Austin just above the ravine

propped up by a boulder. The honeymoon couple
celebrate with a photo.

Tell you this, we're a lucky pair –
my father hands it to me fifty years later.

– Everything which was then the future
was propped up by that boulder.

None of us would have been
but for a stone.

How did it come to be there, that particular
wedding present?

How many such moments are there
hidden in the folds of lives

when everything hangs on a precipice?
And how often when things could go either way

is the way they go
into the rose garden?

TRICIA COROB

Out of Bounds

Their out of bounds bedroom
was a grotto where the low sun
squinnied through the nets
and frisked along the dressing table top
sequinning little jars and bottles.

I would tiptoe in
past the dark shadow of the bed-end,
to the three silver shark-infested pools,
reflected from the mirrors
deep into the pink shag-pile.

Then, Amami wave set, moisture cream, Vaseline,
each screwtop gasping off, leaving me
to trawl inside. Dab on their secrets.
London Rouge, Evening in Paris, a swansdown puff,
glossy lipsticks you could slide up and down
inside their golden ferrules
fitting the caps over my finger-ends
until my fingers swelled
and pulling those caps off
held the sound of a sudden indrawn breath.
A grenade beyond the gate.

But it was the enamelled peacock compact
with its hidden spring release
I prized the most,
examining its fluorescent blues and greens,
each feather's silky eye
and, inside the lid, freckled with powder,
my own unblinking eye
enlarging and enlarging
as I brought the mirror closer,
this third eye, isolate,
staring over my shoulder at the open door.

PRISCILLA BORTHWICK

The Tale of Me

The child's teeth click against the marble.
Her ear is crushed cold against the slab,
The dredged flour almost brushed by her hair.
She traces with her eye her mother's hand.

The hand squashes flour and eggs to hide the yeast
And again it folds and wraps away
The breathing, slackening, raw loaf
That tried to grow and was twisted and turned back –

Like the man in the next room
Wrapped as Adam in broad leaves,
Hiding under the folded mountains that fell on him
When he called them to come and cover him over.

He lies folded around
The pain salting his belly and gut,
Lies still groaning: I am not I,
My story is knotted and
Sour like the bread she made.

EILÉAN NÍ CHUILLEANÁIN

My Father's Shadow

At Seascale our shoes were full of sand.
Daddy emptied them out on the front porch
and we went up the stairs like good girls
and pulled the quilts over our heads as
the rocks dragged the darksilk sea back
over the wet ridged sand again
and again and the sea was lovely really.

Mother said, *It's not cold really,*
you'll get used to it, but I was frightened.
Daddy said, *She'll go in when she's ready.*
He found a hollow in the sand
and something sweet in his pocket.

I wouldn't have chosen to grow up
quite this way, to be quite so far out,
to become so used to the cold
that now I can even lie down in the snow
and imagine it's warm. Imagine
I'm in the warm sand
in the shadow of my father.

DOROTHY NIMMO

158

Wardrobes

My father's womb,
raw wood inside, rough to the touch,
where I crawled to see the album,
khaki squares of men in Singapore
eagled at each corner, hushed in tissue.
Trouser bottoms flapped around my head,
fat envelope of love letters, rent books.
'Sex, Love and Eugenics' curtained by ties.
Mothballs fell like fruit into my lap.

My mother's – larger, bosomy,
polished, dark wood door
inhabited by a bulk of sulking fur,
dovetailed pleated skirts, handbags roosting.
Troops of shoes allowed no chance of wriggling in.
The day she left
I wandered, a bear,
huge cuffs my foraging paws, rattling hangers,
miles, in the echoing, empty bellied wood.

NICOLETTE GOLDING

The Pulse

If the heart is a house my parents
live there separated by a wall.

Tall rooms are secretly linked
by long muscular stairs, a pyramid

of light I travel up to the point
of their joining. If only I could see

under their door the glowing bubble
the light comes from, the quick pulse

at the centre beating like concussion:
the hidden verb of their talk.

In a lit corner of the hall
I can see their two bodies bend

apart like a river forking.
Hear their neat footsteps pause

on the turning-point of the stairs.
An exact door clicks.

Then the dark house makes
untranslated language in the night:

pound and pound, pound,
overheard from my bed.

MARTHA KAPOS

That Rank Bed

That rank bed,
my father only made lance-corporal.
Winceyette sheets,
my mother said sex hurts.
Why did I seek a place between
their humps of back-to-back
those childish half-clothed mornings?

He was hirsute,
she would not wear his hairiness,
she fitted her hernia behind a rosy belt
Coils of thick pink piping,
some strange baby-cord,
dangled around holes
where babies start as lumps.

Wedlocked they worked
a double bed,
a loveless garden
where vows had gone to seed.
The child I was
still runs from the cold hours
to squeeze between them.

That rank breath,
the smell of fetid flowers
require some rare conception,
some orchidaceous thing.
Over and over I try
to unearth an aestuous stem
to heal heartlands
laid waste in winceyette,
to salvage them.

NADINE BRUMMER

Where Are You?

In this garden, after a day of rain,
a blackbird is taking soundings,
flinging his counter-tenor line
into blue air, to where
an answering cadenza shows
the shape and depth of his own solitude.

Born in South London, inheritors
of brick, smoke, slate, tarmac,
uneasy with pastoral
as hill-billies with high-rise,
my parents called each other
in blackbird language:
my father's interrogative whistle
– 'where are you?'
my mother's note, swooping, dutiful
– 'here I am'.

There must have slid into the silences
the other questions,
blind, voiceless worms whose weight
cluttered his tongue;
questions I hear as, half a lifetime on,
I eavesdrop on blackbirds.

CAROLE SATYAMURTI

Love Letters

Alone at home one afternoon
I found them in my father's desk.
A bolted fortress, as a rule –
But now a drawer yielded,
There they lay, ribboned
And stacked in one elaborate box:
Letters my parents had received
Before their marriage.

Strange sympathy I felt
For that young Christian girl
His mother disapproved of –
For many years her lines
Had burnt and cradled him.
Hers were the only ones he'd kept.

But on my mother's side
A pot-pourri of males:
Some officers in trenches
Shimmering with her praises
Written in muddy misery.
Another she'd made eyes at
From a theatre box;
One, a Black Forest holiday friend
Who even called her 'bride' –
All pleading on their paper knees!

Like pickles they had been preserved
Inside this occult box
Not seeing daylight much,
Not for a daughter's eyes.

LOTTE KRAMER

The Mistress

She put away her hats,
the deep-crowned felts and straws
that had housed her bun of hair.
Marcelled and shingled
she seemed to shed spinsterhood
almost be made anew.

At first it had been a cushioned lap,
a hand I reached up to hold,
the angle of familiar feet –
strap shoes with louis heels.
I knew her busy step, opaque stockings,
plain serge skirts. And then one Christmas
a dress of dove-grey marocain,
low-sashed; a long necklace,
dangling, tasselled. She smelled
of lavender and vanishing cream.

Once, I believe, I glimpsed her naked
through a half-open door.

Partisan daughter, I learned to resent
the auntish gifts that had bribed my childhood
so easily – sweets, stamps, pennies;
began to see how sycophancy worked
on a vain man's heart; knew why
my mother would sometimes shrug away
my father's hand, would flinch
from a compliment as from a sting.

PAMELA GILLILAN

Shipping the Pictures from Belfast

She left then, spitting the reek of soil
on dockside's crusted slabs.

He left, watching the gantries of the yards
sink against sunset, and the channels burn.
Saw tubes of cadmium red, alizarin
worm onto his palette, too late for use.

Their props trussed up for shipping
across the water: his were
      maps with the scrim worn clean
      at foldings, pastel directories
      of his restless love that sought
      always another version
      of Ulster's light. The paintings,
      too, in their crate.

And hers?
      Albums of sharp-toned
      snaps, faces in close-up
      that blocked out
      vistas, the picturesque.
      Looming large, her living
      darlings. And herself
      resolute madonna
      back firm set to rocks
      lovelier than Leonardo's.

CATHERINE BYRON

'Why is this night different from all other nights?'
('Ma Nishtana . . . ?')

When there's a hint of spring, and the first crocus
begins its small festival return
to catch a whiff of smoke at the kitchen door.

Observe the flames from silver candlesticks
how one is steady whilst another shivers
round a curled wick and may have to be snuffed.

Check the green dish with its small compartments
for parsley, shank bone and the puttybrown paste
of nuts and wine. You're twelve in the country
of metaphor; as the youngest present recite
the 'Ma Nishtana' to begin the story.

Now admire your father who's decided to sing
like Gigli. Dip your finger in wine
to spatter ten drops on a plate, one at a time
and intone after him the ten plagues.

You may pull the tab in the blue Haggada.
Open the windows, one at a time, on the frogs
the spotted people, the sheep upside down.
Was there a scene of blood on doorposts?
Recall the Egyptian children. Now reflect

on the room, how it's scrubbed and swept clean
of the last Hovis crumb. It's time for the meal,
so break a matzah in two and crush a hardboiled egg
into saltwater prepared by your father.

Can't you hear, as always, your mother nag
that there's much too much salt?
Watch your father go red and the vein in his forehead throb;
but don't rush out of the door because the night
isn't that different. Piece together the scene
in the cut glass of a decanter. Taste the richness
of the cement – re-work a wall from wine and almonds.

And write a new story:
your parents sit bowed in the sand, weary
of pyramids toppling over, the hauling
of slabs for pharaohs. Pretend
that you're Moses, the child they expected.

Take hold of their hands, his where dark hair
sprouts at his wrists, hers where the knuckles are rubbed
by a dishwater sea. Don't stay where you don't belong –
take them out of your childhood

to the land everyone's promised.
Leave them in peace, and stay at the border yourself
feeding off manna.

NADINE BRUMMER

Love

The right words elude me
blurt shamefaced
I was a horrid child,
and must have hurt you in my teens . . .
bad-tempered, back-answering . . .
Your eyes look puzzled, dry of tears –
No, you were a lovely girl . . .

Conscience holds the mirror
to my sharp-eyed memory
shows much I'd sooner miss
will always recognise.
Thank you for not sharing
my memories; forgiving me,
and being so much more than blind

but all the same,
I apologise . . .

JOAN GORDON

God Is Dead – Nietzsche

Daddy and I are always here, you know,
Whenever you want us.
We didn't like the things you said
The last time home.
Bourgeois, you said, and a word which sounded
Very like atrophied.
Daddy doesn't like the way you collect
Toilet graffiti,
God is dead – Nietzsche, and the reply,
Nietzsche is dead – God.

You can't expect Daddy to go round
With the plate in church
With thoughts like that in his head.
I worry too.
Structuralism sounds like a building-site,
Semiology sounds rather rude
In a medical kind of way.
The dogs are well, both almost human,
As we've often said
To you.

Please wear a vest, the days are getting
Colder. We hope you will not be so rude
The next time home.
Daddy and I have just re-done your room.
The blood on the wall hardly shows
After two coats of paint.
Cambridge must be very pretty just now.
I am, in spite of everything,
Your loving Mother.

ELIZABETH BARTLETT

Confrontation with a Bouquet

Flowers. Masquerading as words.
To say *They* know I'm here.
But – swaddled in cellophane,
wreathed in ribbon.
Stifled.
Clean.

So many varieties!
So many tones and nuances!
Gagged by alternatives
I daren't touch one.

Then the whole ward cracks
into questions like shrapnel.
Be safe. So I ram the bouquet
headfast in the bin – but
a nurse jumps up to save it.
Cluck-cluck. Mum.
Nurse splits it, she doesn't know,
and so there are –

    red roses in the recesses
    white wallflowers on the windowsills
    loose lilies in the lavatory
    prim poppies in the office
    all the voices screaming!

I can't go near.
Unless I'm sure.
Are they bits of me?
Or are they bits of *Them*?

Now they're widening their mouths
into prophets who'll relate
the story of a girl . . .

But I can't hear it.
The message is subliminal.
And what if? What if?
What if they've got it wrong?

I pray and pray all day.
But no-one will ordain me
the Okay to ask them
to speak up and explain.

So in the middle of the night
I go and seize them hostage.
They gape incredulous as Judas
when I tell them who I am.

MAGGIE BEVAN

Matching Flowers

Hotpink crimplene petunias,
sashaying down the street,
cheap pyjama striped
in toothpaste white.

He's a regular guy,
his meaty arm sizzling
with gold wire, purple
jeans, pink singlet
netting his bearded chest,
his white grin beamed
at the flowers, bunched
like a lamb frill at his wrists.

Fifty years ago
my father crushed
my mother's gift
into his tool bag,
swung it nonchalantly
from the tip
of his banana hand.

Tossed on the table,
crushed labials
of wallflowers spoke
dark sweetness in the kitchen.

'They're squashed!'
she said bitterly,
her red hair flattened
in the steam.

He shrugged, spun
his trilby on the settee.
A fag, thin as cotton thread
bloomed in his cupped hand.

Bruised green stems,
dead pheasant gold,
wine red, bled a little
on the oilcloth.

I envy the man
with matching flowers
his heart's panache.

My Father's timid thumbs
ached for the feel
of dark red petals.

KATE FOLEY

Taking Tea with My Father and Mother

He takes Earl Grey tea
without milk.
It looks like light brown tizer
in the green glass cup.

The sitting room
is clean and tidy.
It has white walls
a polished Louis Quinze table
a polished Queen Anne bookcase
a polished Biedermeier bureau
floor length, paprika-coloured, velvet curtains
to hide the distant sounds of screaming
coming from the bureau.

Somewhere inside
the second or third drawer down
if he turns the key
and pulls the drawer out
just far enough for it to tip
is an old leather folder with letters.
The tiny brown button inside
keeps the silence.

In the cubicle
the roof is so low
he can't stand up
he can't sit
the seat is so narrow.

Is she still
in the women's cell?

A white sky hangs
outside the long sash window.

Sitting opposite him
she eats Danish pastry
sips her tea.

He sits quietly
in his maroon leather slippers.

On the bureau
watching from their photograph
his grandchildren
know the side of him
that can dance.

PAM ZINNEMANN-HOPE

NOTE: The cubicle refers to my parents'
imprisonment in the Stalin purges of 1937.

One Flesh

Lying apart now, each in a separate bed,
He with a book, keeping the light on late,
She like a girl dreaming of childhood,
All men elsewhere – it is as if they wait
Some new event: the book he holds unread,
Her eyes fixed on the shadows overhead.

Tossed up like flotsam from a former passion,
How cool they lie. They hardly ever touch,
Or if they do it is like a confession
Of having little feeling – or too much.
Chastity faces them, a destination
For which their whole lives were a preparation.

Strangely apart, yet strangely close together,
Silence between them like a thread to hold
And not wind in. And time itself's a feather
Touching them gently. Do they know they're old,
These two who are my father and my mother
Whose fire from which I came, has now grown cold?

ELIZABETH JENNINGS

One Flesh

'She was all woman, all women to me.'
This, after we'd washed her at the hospital, and she'd pleaded
to come home, though he hadn't made a ramp
for her wheelchair yet, and she couldn't get her false teeth in
to eat, her gums jumping with the crab
that had settled itself all over.

'I'm going to die tonight,' she'd said, as he held her from behind
for comfort. He held the tea-cup to her lips and countered
'Don't be daft.' 'I am, I am,' she whispered.
He called to tell me in the morning.

I'd thought my parents' marriage
the usual pain, rocking on
through years of compromise and waste.
The flowers he brought her home from work,
his kiss as she leant against the oven
I thought an obligation.

I wasn't ready for his 'She was all woman, all women to me':
my needful, salutary exclusion from their marriage.

JULIA CASTERTON

Chords

Saturday, March the first, she rings;
Her voice is so low, I strain to hear.
'How are you, love? I prayed when I heard
of the Moorgate crash, that you were O.K.'
'I'm fine, I'm sorry I didn't phone.'
Guilt-ridden, twine the cord round my finger.
'Who is it?' yells Kate. 'Just my mother!'
'I've done a novena for you,' she confides,
'to keep you safe.' Our doorbell chimes.
'I'll have to go, I'll call you later.'
'All right dear, God bless.' I break the connection;
forget her again. Next week, the line's dead.

Sunday, March the first, I ring
to tell him of yesterday's City explosion.
'I'm fine' he bellows, 'what did you say?
A bomb! What bomb? I never read the papers!'
Knot the cord round his throat; I miss her, I'm choked.
'It could have killed me.' Each word a stone.
'Then you'd better change your accent' he jokes.
I grip the receiver; I'd like to rip
the cord from its roots; sever the line.
I long for my mother. But it's
too late now! Next week, he'll chide:
'Do you know it's been seventeen years since she died?'

EAMER O'KEEFFE

178

Easter Outing

The first, delicate apple-greens,
the near-orange tips of pollarded willows
along the water meadow, the virgin whites
of blackthorn and cherry on the slopes. Spring.

Since they can only shuffle and wince a few steps
I drive my parents into the steep valley.
April still holds its delight for them – just –
but all excitement's gone. Perhaps they sense

they should die now: within this last year
of a last decade. Their history
passed, their geography, science, beliefs –
dignity even. They're sad, though they don't say so.

I look at them, swaddled, bent. See again
those newsprint elders, confused and weeping
with hunger and grief this Easter
in the water meadows of the Lepenec . . .

I, too, would've had to wheel them in barrows
to the train: hips and spines repeatedly jarred
so they cried out like the children and babes.
I, too, could've given no succour.

Their agony would've echoed the length
of the packed coaches. Out into the bridal
countyside, amongst smouldering pyres
of barns and homes. Echoed down the century.

SALLY CARR

Rings *

Before my mother left she lost both rings,
first between the sheets, then in the cracks
beneath the borrowed hospice crib. These rings
my father found by feel and safely kept

until the funeral. That day he gave
each daughter's daughter one: the elder, gold,
the younger, silver with a diamond ray,
and told the story of the purchase, and showed

his band so that we saw the thicker golden
braided mate and saw my father's knuckle
thickened with arthritis. We four crowded
close. Gleaming clippers snapped the metal.

Then we saw my father shake his head
and stare at his bare hand. 'She's gone,' he said.

JOAN MICHELSON

* from a sequence, 'Departures'

Cat's-Cradle

Replacing rings on her hands,
treading circles, the tight route
between bedsheets and washing-machine,
sometimes cleaning the already clean

she stitches absences, tracing where his bulk
had been, his fishing-hat still perched
on a shelf, as if he lives on
and she is the ghost, rehearsing

a role that no longer exists,
its shell grown hard, still netting
the seed that stirs in her,
a girlish wistfulness in her eyes,

the solo moon of her face
looking out through diamond panes,
their half-chosen limitations,
as if her hands, rubbing the glass,

can't quite pierce the dream
while she stands, almost content,
at the soothing loom of ritual,
cat's-cradles of love and memory

touching a secret I fail to grasp,
her hands, pleated by detergent,
feeling plates' familiar rims,
their sparkling, half-drowned shapes.

LYNNE WYCHERLEY

Two Statues

We stood, my mother and I,
two frozen statues
on the edge of a man-made lake.
Unable to comfort each other
in good times, with death
sitting in the house,
we kept apart.
Our cold grief locked within.

The sculptured smooth façade
lasting our lifetime.

And father lay in the lounge
on that first morning of his death.
His stubble had grown over night.
Like a threshing of mushrooms
an act of defiance through the
starved skin.

Mother took a knife and shaved him.
Cutting away the black dew.
I watched from the doorway
hypnotised by actions
I had no space for.
She held his body, I his soul.

Two statues sitting on a mantlepiece.
The light from the fire
catching our fading colours,
we grew old.
Facing each other.
Our cold grief locked within.

PAULINE HAWKESWORTH

The Photograph

has fixed my mother and father in a garden
I know by heart though I've not entered it
for years. A sharper mirror than water, it insists
on their solidity, claims they will shine for ever.
As I look a longing I can't call love stops up
my throat and I'm shocked that each parent
is thinner than card, than one of the scrawled
white sheets lying on my desk – is nothing
I can touch in a rosebed labelled remembrance.
Yet here they sit on a gleaming bench, brighter
than life, presenting smiles to the world.
Her summer dress is dappled mauve and blue,
he's in his best suit, handkerchief peeping.
Behind them by the hedge with the iron-runged gate
I opened so often to dream among the raspberries
and broad beans, unrestrained phlox
offer exuberant heads . . .

'Don't be stupid!' My father's fist lands
on his spindly diagrams of electric circuits.
Spring is trying to climb in the window
and my sixteen-year-old self aches to jump
out to beech-leaf sunlight, out of disgrace
for not understanding, making undrinkable tea,
never sitting up straight at table. And now
my mother is slapping crockery into the sink
because he's too busy to go on a picnic.
Suddenly both are throwing bricks of rage
and that faint, wavering self pulls back
the screams threatening to leap from her head,
terrified she'll be struck into madness . . .

Banish these two, sink the garden?
I'd wipe out my path from then to now,
lose myself. I need to recover the time
when darkheart leaves, the wind running
through young wheatfields were too perfect
to bear, to recapture my mother playing the piano,
stooping to name a small flower on the Downs,

that walk from humming stubble heat into
the blur of evening when we were in tune
and she said: 'Your mind is beautiful'. I need to find
my father – the excitement we shared as he gave me
glimpses into the strange country of mathematics,
its patterns, laws, the invisible dimension occupied
by the square and potent root of minus one
which burgeoned wildly in my dreams at night. If I sit
with my parents on their bench will angers cease
and the soft salt waters of forgiveness rise?

MYRA SCHNEIDER

Arioso Dolente

For my grandchildren when they become grandparents

Mother, who read and thought and poured herself into me;
she was the jug and I was the two-eared cup.
How she would scorn today's 'show-biz inanity,
democracy twisted, its high ideals sold up!'
              Cancer filched her voice, then cut her throat.
                     Why is it
       none of the faces in this family snapshot
                looks upset?

Father, who ran downstairs as I practised the piano;
barefooted, buttoning his shirt, he shouted 'G,
D-natural, C-*flat! Dolente, arioso.*
Put all the grief of the world in that change of key.'
            Who then could lay a finger on his sleeve
                    to distress him with
       'One day, Steve, two of your well-taught daughters
                will be deaf.'

Mother must be sitting, left, on the porch-set,
you can just see her. My sister's on her lap.
And that's Steve confiding to his cigarette
something my mother's mother has to laugh at.
           The screened door twangs, slamming
                on its sprung hinge.
           Paint blisters on the steps; iced tea, grasscuttings,
                elm flowers, mock orange . . .

A grand June evening, like this one, not too buggy,
unselfquestioning midwestern, maybe 1951.
And, of course, there in my grandmother's memory
lives just such another summer – 1890 or 1891.
           Though it's not on her mind now/then.
              No, she's thinking of
       the yeast-ring rising in the oven. Or how *any* shoes
                irritate her bunion.

Paper gestures, pictures, newsprint laughter.
And after the camera winks and makes its catch,
the decibels drain away *for ever and ever.*
No need to say 'Look!' to these smilers on the porch,
              'Grandmother will have her stroke,
                          and you, mother, will nurse her.'
       Or to myself, this woman died paralyzed–dumb, and that one
                          dumb from cancer.

Sufficient unto the day . . . Grandmother, poor and liturgical,
whose days were duties, stitches in the tea-brown blanket
she for years crocheted, its zig-zag of yellow wool,
her grateful offering, her proof of goodness to present,
              gift-wrapped, to Our Father in Heaven. 'Accept,
                          O Lord, this best-I-can-make-it-soul.'
       And He: 'Thou good and faithful servant, lose thyself
                          and be whole.'

Consciousness walks on tiptoe through what happens.
So much is felt, so little of it said.
But ours is the breath on which the past depends.
'What happened' is what the living teach the dead,
              who, smilingly lost to their lost concerns,
                          in gray on grey,
              are all of them deaf, blind, unburdened
                          by today.

As if our recording selves, our mortal identities,
could be cupped in a concave universe or lens,
ageless at all ages, cleansed of memories,
not minding that meaningful genealogy extends
              no further than mind's flash images reach back.
                          As for what happens next,
                   let all the griefs of the world
                          find keys for that.

ANNE STEVENSON

---

* Arioso dolente, from Beethoven's piano sonata, opus 110, third movement;
introduction to the fugue.

Beachy Head

I see you now, my mother and father,
Coming up this cliff slowly, though you did
So but yesterday, as if you are long dead.
Here my father, placing his legs askew
As he pulls for breath, turns to look back
Down the twisting path they have come.
My mother touches her arthritic knee.
And all around, the great arc of the world
Encloses them. O keep back from the dazzling edge,
Daddy, don't move with your vertigo closer
To the drop, the terrible slippage.
Lay out your provisions and go giddy
With the clouds running overhead.
And my mother unwraps the boiled eggs,
Lets tea from the thermos, lies down close
To the ticking grass while across to France
The years flash back and forth
With their insistent whisper, hish, hish,
Lullaby, wash away our hurt down the shingle;
How these two rheumaticky people shimmer
Like gods in the grass.

HILARY DAVIES

Biographical Notes
compiled by Dilys Wood

ANNA ADAMS spends time in London and North Yorkshire. 'I wrote only intermittently until, in 1960, I suffered a life-threatening illness. Then I put my back into writing poetry, enjoying the discipline of form. My first published pieces were prose and it was seven years before my first published poem, "An Eye Donor".' Peterloo brought out her first collection, *A Reply to Intercepted Mail* in 1979. This was followed by *Dear Vincent* (Littlewood Press) and *Trees in Sheep Country* (Peterloo) in 1986, *Nobodies* (Peterloo), 1990, *Island Chapters* (Littlewood Press), 1991, *Life on Limestone* (Smith Settle), 1993 (the last two are mainly prose). Two collections of poetry came out in 1996 – *Green Resistance, New and Selected Poems* (Enitharmon) and *A Paper Ark* (Peterloo). In 1999 Enitharmon published *Thames*, her anthology of poems about the river Thames.

PATRICIA ADELMAN lives in Bath. 'I began writing poems in the late 1980s after a life-time of other kinds of work – shop assistant, nanny, pit-canteen hand, trainee nurse, wife, mother, primary school teacher, English teacher, with the study necessary for the teaching (my grammar-school education was aborted at fourteen). As long as I can remember, poetry has at least nudged my attention and I have derived the utmost pleasure from teaching poetry appreciation and composition.' She has a substantial number of poems published in magazines and a pamphlet, *Life, Still Life and a Few Stones*, but says, 'Born in the 1930s and brainwashed by the culture of the work ethic, I still battle with myself to allow prime time for writing poetry and to feel the effort justified.'

MONIZA ALVI lives in London. 'I was born in Pakistan in 1954 and grew up in Hertfordshire. My first two collections, *The Country at My Shoulder* and *A Bowl of Warm Air*, were published by Oxford University Press, and a new collection is due from Bloodaxe. Writing poetry has enabled me to explore and come to terms with the difficulties and pleasures of growing up as a girl with a racially mixed background. I am pleased that there are some marvellous women writers with multi-cultural backgrounds who have inspired me and who will be there for the poets of the future.'

FRANCES ANGELA lives in London. 'I am a fifty-year-old woman. I left school at fifteen and worked in a number of jobs including mill and shop work. In my early twenties I trained as a social worker specialising in mental health and worked with children. When my son was born I took up photography and studied for a degree. Through self-portraiture I worked on the subject of identity, exploring issues of class, mental health, sexuality and gender. I believe that these issues inform my poetry which I began to write in my mid-forties.'

R. V. BAILEY lives in Gloucestershire. She was born in Northumberland, educated at Whitley Bay Grammar School and Girton College, Cambridge and her main career has been teaching English at Cheltenham Ladies' College,

College of St Matthias, Bristol and the University of the West of England. She has further degrees, University College, Swansea (Dip.S.C.) and University of Oxford (D.Phil.). 'I wrote poetry as a student; began writing seriously later because I had to teach students creative writing and they wouldn't let me get away without joining in . . .' Her first collection is *Course Work* (Culverhay Press, 1997). She reviews for *The North* and *Envoi* and has given poetry readings with U. A. Fanthorpe, whose poetry Audiotapes, *Double Act* (Penguin), and *Poetry Quartets 5* (Bloodaxe) include Bailey's voice.

JILL BAMBER lives in London. 'I started to write in my fifties after a lifetime spent bringing up a family, two marriages, four sons and an art school background. I earned my living as an Occupational Therapist and write about relationships, finding that writing helps me achieve a clearer idea of my role as older woman and grandmother.' She has four books published: the latest is *Touch Paper* from Aramby Wire. She became Blue Nose Poet of the Year in 1997-8 and is a contact person for Highgate Poets, regularly editing their annual anthology *Kites*, now in its twentieth year.

WANDA BARFORD lives in London. She was born in Italy, in Milan, during the Mussolini era and emigrated as a child to Zimbabwe. 'I studied music at the Royal College but my first love was literature, particularly poetry. Compelled to earn a living teaching the piano, I did not put poetry in the centre of my life until my late-fifties.' She has been widely published in magazines, anthologies, and newspapers, such as the *Independent, Observer, Daily Express, Tablet* and *Jewish Chronicle*, and has published two collections, *Sweet Wine and Bitter Herbs* and *A Moon at the Door*. A third, *Losing, Finding* is forthcoming.

CELIA BARRY lives in Sussex. 'I began my career as an artist and married an artist. I moved to Hong Kong, exhibiting with the British Council in 1959, then moved to Scotland, continuing to paint while bringing up three children. An Open University humanities degree (1971-76) was followed by part-time English teaching. After my children left school I began writing poetry more seriously and took up calligraphy as a method of studying and absorbing poems. Poetry gives the varied things I do, such as gardening, walking and travelling, a double purpose.' Her poems have been published in *Southern Arts Magazine, The Tablet, Envoi* and *Manifold*.

ELIZABETH BARTLETT lives in West Sussex. 'To me poetry is a vocation. I left grammar school at fifteen. My first poem was published by *Poetry London* when I was eighteen. I did not have a collection published until I was fifty-five, when Harry Chambers of Peterloo invited me to send. *A Lifetime of Dying* was published. I am now seventy-five and still writing.' Her *New and Selected Poems, Two Women Dancing* was published in 1995 by Bloodaxe, and Bloodaxe are shortly to bring out a new collection.

MAGGIE BEVAN lives in Wales. 'I was recently granted a New Writer's Bursary from the Welsh Arts Council. I teach English in schools and creative writing for Mind and have become increasingly involved in giving/organising poetry readings and workshops.' She has published poems in a range of magazines and anthologies, including *Poetry Wales, Acumen, The Gregory Poems* (Penguin), *The Long Pale Corridor* (Bloodaxe), *Hard Lines* (Faber).

PATRICIA BISHOP lives in Gloucestershire. 'I have always loved poetry, been obsessed by it, but have only been writing for ten or eleven years. During that time I have been widely published in magazines and anthologies and, in addition to minor prizes, came second in the National Poetry Competition, 1994. An Arts Council/BBC award also led to me broadcasting my poems on Radio 3. My poetry has also been on Radio 4 and various local stations, and, when living in Cornwall, I was poet-in-residence to Penwith libraries for five years.' Her publications include, *Double Exposure* (Westwords) and *Aubergine is a Gravid Woman* (Headland). Her third collection is *Saving Dragons* (Oversteps Books, 2000).

GILLIE BOLTON lives near Sheffield in the Hope Valley. Her latest collection is *Hole in the Moon* (Waldean Press, 1997). She edits a poetry page for two academic medical journals. She works with doctors, nurses and therapists in using creative writing to reflect deeply upon their work. Her *Reflective Practice Writing for Professional Development: Stories at Work*, is due for publication in 2000 by Sage Publications. She supports patients to write creatively and therapeutically and trains health clinicians in this work (*The Therapeutic Potential of Creative Writing: Writing Myself*, Jessica Kingsley Publishers, 1999). 'The work with others has been made possible from making therapeutic use of creative writing myself: poems like "Little Red Riding Hood" exemplify what greater maturity enables me to do.'

ANNE BORN lives in South Devon. 'Early marriage, university and children took up most time until my fourth and last child was three but poetry has always been of the greatest importance in my professional life. I work as a full-time literary translator, mainly of fiction but also of poetry, and this is an exciting extension for a poet. "Poetry is the music of what happens", says Seamus Heaney, and you try to catch notes of that music when you write. Like music, poetry is joyful, sad, loud, calm, thunderous or gentle – and witty, and fun. The best moment is when you get a genuine laugh from the audience! It was a particular joy that my late husband, who had never been interested in poetry, eventually came to like some of my poems'. *Planting Light* (Headland, 1999) is her latest collection.

PRISCILLA BORTHWICK lives in Yorkshire. 'I trained in fine art and went on to take a diploma in ceramic sculpture, with work now in public collections. In 1989 and 2000, I won Yorkshire Arts Writer's Bursaries. In 1990 my first full-length collection was published by Littlewood Press. I have had three further pamphlet collections published and a new full-length collection, *Hospital Corners*, is due out in 2000.' Her short stories and poems are widely published. She is a part-time tutor in Creative Writing for Leeds University. She has been Writer in Residence in prisons, schools, libraries, hospitals and hospices and, following her stint in 1997 as Writer in Residence for the Chesterfield Canal, her 400 ft long poem 'still glows from inside Drakeholes Tunnel'.

JEAN BINTA BREEZE divides her time between Jamaica and London. She has published three main poetry collections, *Riddym Ravings* (Race Today, 1988), *Spring Cleaning* (Virago Press, 1992) and *On the Edge of an Island* (Bloodaxe, 1997), as well as several records, including the album, *Trades,* with the Dennis Bovell Dub Band. She has performed her work throughout the world, including tours of the Carribean, N. America, Europe, South East Africa and Asia.

PAM BRIDGEMAN lives in Cumbria. 'I was born in 1950. I teach English in a Sixth Form College and am an Associate Lecturer for the Open University. My first published poem was in *Iron* magazine when I was thirty-four. I was awarded a Northern Arts Writer's Award in 1997 which encouraged me to put together a first collection, now doing the rounds. I also received a Northern Arts Travel Award in 1999 which furthered a sequence of poems based on the Italian experiences of Mary Shelley and Frieda Lawrence. The part writing plays in my life is well-expressed by the Canadian poet Louis Dudek, "The writing of poetry is a lot like being in love" and the act of writing is, "A state of peculiar concentration, an ecstasy." She is widely published in magazines and anthologies.

JACQUELINE BROWN lives near Sheffield in the Hope Valley. 'Born in 1944 in West Yorks, I began writing as a child of five – academic work then took over and it was not until the early 1980s that I began writing seriously. Poetry is not easy. It requires a dive into the inner self which can sometimes be disturbing, but there is nothing to beat the feeling of having produced something new and as perfect as one can make it.' Her collections include, *Accidental Reality* (Littlewood Press), *Thinking Egg,* winner of the Arvon/Observer prize and *In a Woman's Likeness* (a Poetry Book Society Recommendation) – the last two were published by Arc Publications.

NADINE BRUMMER lives in London. 'I was born in Manchester to Jewish parents of Eastern European immigrant stock – the first from a large extended family to go to university, winning an exhibition to Somerville. Illness prevented me completing Greats at Oxford, but later, while in full-time teaching, I took a Philosophy degree at Birkbeck College, University of London. After several years as a psychiatric social worker, I was appointed lecturer and Tutor at Goldsmiths College. Writing poetry came late. My first published poem was in *New Poetry 4* (PEN/Hutchinson). Writing and submitting work were sporadic until early retirement.' A first chapbook collection, *A Question of Blue Tulips and Other Poems,* was published by Shoestring Press in 1999.

SUZANNE BURROWS lives in Hertfordshire. 'I have been writing poetry for the last ten years. I have been a prize-winner in the Bridport and Ver poetry competitions. My first collection of poems, *The Dream Garden,* was published by Campion in 1998.'

CATHERINE BYRON lives in Leicester. 'I was born in 1947 and grew up in Belfast, child of an English father and a Southern Irish mother. I studied medieval literature at Somerville. My mongrel inheritance lay dormant until my late thirties, when insistent dreams summoned me to the West of Ireland to write *Galway*, a sequence of poems based on my grandmother's life (Settlements, 1985 and 1993). Once a farmer myself, I continue to write about the violence women and men visit on each other and on the animate and inanimate natural world. I have recently written about my parents' mixed marriage in "The Most Difficult Door" (*Women's Lives Into Print*, ed. P. Polkey, Macmillan, 1999).' In 1997 she received an ACE Writer's Award. Her latest collection is *The Getting of Vellum* (Salmon/Blackwater).

SALLY CARR lives in Wiltshire. 'Writing is my way of making some sense of life, recording, analysing, forcing myself to find words. I am a poet who usually needs umpteen drafts. I started writing when my children were small as something I could do while they were asleep or at playschool. I had previously taught poetry. I won the Bridport prize in 1993 with a poem which was the direct upshot of a traumatic time in family life. I have had more than eighty poems published in magazines and anthologies. It took a long time and a hard slog to reach the milestone of a first collection – many editors saw my poems as "too quiet", "too domestic".' Her first collection, *Electrons on Bonfire Night*, was published in 1997, by Rockingham Press. A second collection, *The Memory Ocean*, is nearing completion.

LIZ CASHDAN lives in Sheffield. 'I teach Creative Writing at Derby University and Sheffield University. Two shared publications from Smith/Doorstep are *Troublesome Cattle* and *Almost Like Talking*. The most recent is *Laughing All the Way* (Five Leaves, 1995). At the moment I am working with batik and digital-image artist Pat Hodson to produce poetry and images that complement each other. I started writing when a secondary school English teacher and realised that I couldn't teach writing without being a writer. Just now I am doing some research into women writers of the Romantic period – 300 women poets in print in 1800 and even more novelists and travel writers. They are my writing grandmothers, so it's ironic that the editors of this anthology have chosen a poem about my father!'

JULIA CASTERTON lives in London. 'I was born near Nottingham in 1952, the eldest of four sisters. The only book prized at home was the Bible – a wonderful start but I was always struggling to find words that could hold the things that happened. After my third sister, Rachel, was killed in a car crash, I looked to writing to help me gather up what was lost. Studying literature at university gave me time to read and think but corseted me in academic analysis. When a young editor asked me to write *Creative Writing: A Practical Guide* (Macmillan, 1986 and 1998) I began to understand the life-saving role writing had played for me, how I had written out of feelings of loss and how I longed to write from a state of joy and plenitude.' Her collections are *That Slut Cleopatra* (Turret Books, 1988), *Troublesome Cattle*, with Liz Cashdan, and *Bottom's Dream* (Smith/Doorstop, 1990 and 1995).

ALISON CHISHOLM lives in Merseyside where she works as a poetry and creative writing tutor and for the BBC's Radio Merseyside as a poetry consultant. 'Poetry has been at the heart of my life since my very early teens, first as a spoken art to gain qualifications in speech and drama, then as the best medium for thoughts and feelings.' She writes articles on poetry for *Writers News, Writing, Springboard, Freelance Market News.* She has written writers' guides, *The Craft of Writing Poetry* and *A Practical Writing Course* (Allison Bury). Her latest poetry collection, *Daring the Slipstream* was published by Headland in 1997.

MOIRA CLARK lives 'in the heart of beautiful Hampshire'. 'Writing is as essential to my life as breathing. Success in my forties has developed into an addiction for words. My first collection, *Stookey Blues & Fat Hen* was published on my forty-eighth birthday. I perform from Edinburgh to Hastings and am well-known for my waistcoats and dickie-bows. My latest achievement is being appointed Poet in Residence with Eastleigh Borough for 2000.' She is preparing her second collection and her poems have been selected for an anthology about the New Forest. She is widely published in magazines and has won competition prizes in this country and Japan.

GILLIAN CLARKE lives in Llandysul, Ceredigion, West Wales. She was born in Cardiff of Welsh-speaking parents. Poet, playwright, editor, tutor of creative writing for all age-groups, from primary school to the Creative Writing M.Phil course at the University of Glamorgan. Her work is studied widely for the GCSE English examination and she is one of six women poets studied for A level in England and Wales. Recent collections of poems include *Collected Poems* (1997) and *Five Fields* (1998), published by Carcanet Press, *Nine Green Gardens, Poems for Aberglasne* (2000) and a new collection for children, *The Animal Wall and Other Poems* (1999), both published by Gomer Press.

ANNE CLUYSENAAR lives on her smallholding in South Wales, 'an Irish poet living in Usk'. 'I teach creative writing at the University of Wales, Cardiff. My father was the Belgian painter, John Cluysenaar. One of his paintings appears on the cover of my New and Selected Poems, *Timeslips* (Carcanet, 1997). *Timeslips* contains a 22-poem sequence, "Vaughan Variations", exploring the work of the poet, Henry Vaughan. I am Secretary of the Usk Valley Vaughan Associ-ation and poetry editor of its yearly journal *Scintilla*. The Society was founded in 1995 by the poet Angela Morton and myself and holds an annual Colloquium near the Breconshire farm where Vaughan worked as a doctor. I am now concentrating on poems about nature, linked with the work of the Usk-born naturalist, Alfred Russel Wallace.' 'Poems of Memory' was first published in *Double Helix* by Anne Cluysenaar and Sybil Hewat (Carcanet/MidNAG, 1982).

CAROL COIFFAIT lives in East Yorkshire. 'Writing has always been a way of making some sense out of events. Now, since retirement, it is much more, a tool I need to use for many reasons, for fellowship and for fun and it's all my own work! I recently wrote and performed in a three-handed verse-play for women, and participated in a multi-media event at Hull Literature Festival. Last year I read in Bridlington Spa by invitation on National Poetry Day and was shortlisted by Blue Nose/Common Ground poets in their Field Days competition.' Widely published in children's and other poetry anthologies and in magazines.

GLADYS MARY COLES runs a literary press, Headland Publications. Her nine collections of poetry include *Leafburners* (1986), *The Glass Island* (1992 and 1994), and *The Land Within* (1999). Her poetry is anthologised by Faber, Virago, Seren, Cassell, the Forward Prizes, and in *Twentieth Century Anglo-Welsh Poetry* (1997). She has edited six anthologies, most recently *The Poet's View: Poems for Paintings* (1996). Her literary work includes two biographies of Mary Webb and editions of Webb's poetry and prose. Radio work includes a BBC Radio 4 *Kaleidoscope* special feature and poems on *Poetry Please!* The winner of numerous poetry competitions, she has received a Welsh Arts Council Writer's Award and the Daily Post Award for Literature. She lectures at Liverpool University and Liverpool John Moores University, and has led courses for Arvon and the Taliesin Trust (Ty Newydd).

TRICIA COROB lives in London. 'I started out as a dancer and received a spine injury so I took degrees in English and Theatre Studies. When there was no longer the discipline of the dancer's life, I sought a sense of order and meaning through writing. However, I often lost the thread. I wanted to nurture other people, it was less easy to give myself permission to be alone in a room writing. Academic teaching was followed by becoming a therapist, then many journeys to study in India. I now teach meditation. In the last two years I have begun to create the circumstances to give writing more energy and time.' She has been published in magazines and anthologies and has a collection, *House of Tides* (Mosaic Press, 1997).

HILARY DAVIES lives in London and is Head of Languages at St Paul's Girls' School. 'I started writing prose at a very early age, but began poetry only after a degree in French/German at Oxford. While still a post-graduate, I founded the magazine *Argo*. I won a Gregory Award in 1983 and the TLS/Cheltenham Festival poetry competition in 1987, with a Hawthornden Fellowship in 1992. My subject matter is not female-oriented and I attach no particular significance to being a woman. Some critics have called me "intellectual", "academic", "metaphysical", "religious" – depending on your point of view, this is a judgment of praise or opprobrium.' Collections are: *The Shanghai Owner Of The Bonsai Shop* (1991) and *In a Valley of This Restless Mind* (1996), both published by Enitharmon Press.

ANGELA DOVE was born in Yorkshire in 1951 and now lives in London's East End where she works as an education consultant. With her partner she has recently formed an organisation, Poetry Works, to promote poetry readings and is particularly pleased with the Cats Night Out Readings at the Poetry Café where unpublished women writers share a platform with established poets. 'I came to writing both early and late with a big gap in between. Writing was very important to me as a child but then I went in a different direction as a theatre designer and actor. I began to write again at a crucial time about four years ago when struggling to come to terms with a difficult childhood.' Her work has been published in magazines with prize-winning poems in the Bridport and other competitions.

JANE DURAN was born in Cuba in 1944. Brought up in the United States and in Chile, she has lived in England since 1966. A pamphlet of her poems, *Boogie Woogie* was published by Hearing Eye in 1991 and a selection of her work appeared in *Poetry Introduction 8* (Faber and Faber, 1993). Her first full collection, *Breathe Now, Breathe*, published by Enitharmon Press, received the 1995 Forward Poetry Prize for Best First Collection.

JEAN EARLE lives near Shrewsbury. 'I published stories and poetry (of a lighter kind) in my twenties and a good deal of journalism with short radio pieces while in my thirties. After marriage and children somehow it all vanished – but not owing to domesticity, I simply lost the urge. In my late sixties this returned in a flood, now relating to poetry of quite a different kind – so urgent that it quite possessed me. I published my first collection, *A Trial of Strength* (Carcanet, 1980) when I was seventy-one. I have not found any masculine or feminine significance in my writing, simply my own way of looking.' *Visiting Light* (Poetry Wales Press, 1987) was a Poetry Book Society Choice. Her *Selected Poems* (1990) and *The Sun in the West* (1995) were both published by Seren.

U. A. FANTHORPE lives in Gloucestershire. She read English at Oxford and went on to become Head of English at Cheltenham Ladies' College. She decided to try to be a writer in 1974. Her first collection, *Side Effects* (1978), was followed by five others from Peterloo Poets. In 1986 King Penguin published *Selected Poems* (published as a hardback by Peterloo), in 1998 came *Double Act*, a Penguin audiobook with R. V. Bailey, and in 2000 *Consequences* (Peterloo). In 1994 she was the first woman nominated for the post of Professor of Poetry at Oxford. Carol Ann Duffy has said of her work, 'U. A. Fanthorpe is a popular poet – reprinted, studied in schools . . . [she has] done much to make poetry accessible . . . able to write deceptively simple poems which enable us to recognise ourselves.'

ELAINE FEINSTEIN lives in London. She says, 'Writing has been essential to my emotional survival. I have lived as a writer since 1980.' She is a poet and novelist and her versions of the Russian poet, Marina Tsvetayeva's poetry have recently been re-issued from Carcanet/OUP. In 1990 she received a Cholmondeley Award for poetry. In 1995 she was the Chairman of Judges for the T. S. Eliot prize. Her *Selected Poems* were published in 1994 by Carcanet. *Daylight* (Carcanet, 1997), was a Poetry Book Society Recommendation. Her latest collection is *Gold* (Carcanet, 2000). She recently published a biography of Pushkin (Weidenfeld and Nicolson) and edited *After Pushkin, Versions by Contemporary Poets* for the Folio Society. She is working on a biography of Ted Hughes.

KATE FOLEY lives in Amsterdam and Suffolk, 'cautiously well-advanced in kicking the work ethic and writing as attentively as I should have done years ago.' 'Early start in writing, aged eleven, late start in publication, aged fifty-five. In between, midwife teacher and a career in conservation leading to the headship of a national archaeological science/conservation laboratory. As someone thoroughly imbued with feminist/lesbian/and now 'grey' issues, I naturally see myself as a 'woman writer' with all that implies both of strength and practical disadvantages. But I can't write a p.c. poem to save my life and to me this is a hopeful sign that poetry takes our politics and our lives further than we dared to hope.' Her collections are *Soft Engineering* (Onlywomen Press, 1994) and *A Year Without Apricots* (Blackwater Press, 1999).

KATHERINE FROST lives in London. 'I may be the last generation of women for whom seriously delayed entry to poetry-writing is the rule. Let us hope so. I proclaimed myself a future poet at seven but recovered the thread only in middle life. Getting going was slow and painstaking – as for many women, workshops have been important in developing confidence and finding appropriate critical support.' She was the winner of the 1994 Poetry Business Competition (which provides for publication) and her first collection *The Sixth Channel* was published by Smith/Doorstop in 1995. She has been widely published in poetry magazines and anthologies, including *Poetry London, Poetry Review*, the second *Virago/Writing Women Anthology* and the Penguin Book of the Twentieth Century in Poetry, *Scanning the Century*.

CYNTHIA FULLER lives in Esh Winning in County Durham. 'Born in 1948 in Kent, I have lived in the North East for twenty years. Writing and publication waited until my sons reached school-age. It was not until around forty that I felt confident enough to make a proper place in my life for writing. Since 1975 I have taught literature and creative writing, often working with women's groups. I edited *Writing Women* for twelve years, and edited and wrote part of a course on women for the National Extension College in 1991. Experience of the Women's Movement gave me a sense of the validity and variety of women's voices and of the extent to which the literary world had ignored them.' Her collections are *Moving towards Light* and *Instructions for the Desert* (Flambard, 1992, 1996).

ANNE-MARIE FYFE was born in County Antrim and now lives in West London. 'My first collection's title *Late Crossing* . . . [hints] at the continual tensions and transitions between concepts of "home" and "here", between the poetic and the practical, between shifting responsibilities, between the personal and the wider world, which are the focus of my writing.' She lectures in English and teaches creative writing at the Richmond-upon-Thames College, organises poetry readings at the Troubadour in Earl's Court, runs the Richmond Poetry Society at Richmond Adult College and is currently researching aspects of contemporary women's writing. Her 'Women and Mother Ireland' has appeared in *Image and Power* (Longman, 1995). *Late Crossing* was published by Rockingham Press in 1999.

JUDY GAHAGAN lives in London. 'I earned my living as an academic psychologist for many years. When my children were independent, I returned to my first love, writing and started writing for publication about ten years ago. I'm published in many journals, have a volume of short stories *Did Gustav Mahler Ski?* published by New Directions, New York, two poetry pamphlets, *Ghosting the*

Cities, When the Whole Mood Changed, both published by Artemis and a collection, *Crossing the Noman's Land* (Flambard, 1999).

KATHERINE GALLAGHER is Australian-born and now lives in London. She is a widely-published poet, translator and poetry tutor. 'I started writing poetry in 1965, encouraged by the burgeoning women's movement with its poetry anthologies and new publishing outlets for women. Poetry has become my life, my way of seeing. In our era, the fight for visibility is common to all poets but it presents special difficulties for women. There's one answer – and that is to keep writing.' Her collection *Passengers to the City* (Hale and Ironmonger, 1985) was shortlisted for the 1986 Australian National Poetry Prize. Her most recent full collection, *Fish-Rings on Water* (Forest Books, 1989) was followed by a pamphlet, *Finding the Prince* (Hearing Eye, 1993). Her next is due from Arc, followed by *Selected Poems* (Salmon).

BLAIR GIBB sadly died while this anthology was in preparation. She was an American from Virginia who was based in this country working for Amnesty International where her responsibilities, including fund-raising, were heavy and entered into with the utmost commitment and enthusiasm. She had many outside interests in addition – these included running in the London Marathon and an ever-increasing interest in writing poetry. She soon made her mark on the poetry scene in London, where her unusual combination of passion and subtlety was widely appreciated and she was in demand to give readings. After her death friends gathered her poems in a collection, *Tom's Diner*, with a launch arranged by John Rety at Torriano.

PAMELA GILLILAN lives in Bristol. 'Wonderful to have achieved late in life an ambition cherished as a child, to be a poet. Writing regained importance after a long interval – about twenty-five years – during which I neither read nor wrote poetry but was absorbed in other forms of creativity. In 1977 I suddenly knew that I'd be able to write again, but found that my poems were very different from anything I'd produced in my teens and twenties. Unsure of myself, I sent some poems to competitions as they'd be judged anonymously. This was in 1979, when I had successes in both the Cheltenham and the Poetry Society Competitions. I'm sure that this led directly to publication with Bloodaxe of my first book, *That Winter*. Bloodaxe have since published three more – my latest collection is *The Rashomon Syndrome* (1998).'

NICOLETTE GOLDING lives in London. 'I began writing poetry four years ago in my forties after a gap of twenty years, my daughters having reached an age which left me more time for myself. I had ideas, imagination, inspiration and a complete lack of confidence. One evening, drunk on wine, I bundled a few poems into an envelope and sent them to a poetry magazine, *Poetry Nottingham International*. Two were accepted. Joining a regular poetry workshop also helped me get started. I continue to get poems published in journals and two have been selected for Poetry on the Buses.'

JOAN GORDON lives in Leeds. 'I started writing after my children left home and found encouragement in Leeds Writers' Circle of which I am a past Chairman. Articles were published and broadcast on *Woman's Hour* and local radio. Bereavement motivated my first published collection of poetry, *Picking Up The Pieces*. Further poetry appeared in magazines, anthologies and a Reform Synagogue Festival Prayer Book. An autobiography followed, *Tango Down the Corridor*. Writing has given me the friendship of fellow-writers and the reward of meeting interesting people at readings.' 'Love' appeared in the anthology *When Prunes were Plums* and the poem was read at the Wakefield Arts Festival.

ANNE GRIMES lives near Lampeter in Wales. 'I have always written poetry, but a move to West Wales in 1975 provided a real stimulus, poetry being highly regarded in Wales. Family and landscape feature largely in my poetry and, though I sometimes write about large public events, I tend to do it from the starting point of the near and the domestic.' She published a small collection, *Heron's Way* (Spectrum Press, 1987) and has since published in magazines such as *Poetry Wales, New Welsh Review, The Interpreter's House, Envoi*.

CATHY GRINDROD lives in Derbyshire. She has been the Editor of *Poetry Nottingham International* since 1996. 'I did not begin writing poetry until six years ago at the age of thirty-two. Until then, life, responsibilities and children came first, although poetry had been an absorbing interest from an early age. Now the writing, teaching and promoting of poetry has taken over my life.' She is widely published in magazines, with a collection, *Something the Heart Can't Hold*, published by the Nottingham Poetry Society.

LUCY HAMILTON lives in Hythe, Kent. 'I started secondary-school teaching in Whitechapel and Brixton in 1973 and ended a twenty-year teaching career in Cambridge. During these years my chief writing outlet was a journal in which I recorded thoughts, feelings, observations and notes about current reading. This constituted a kind of lifeline enabling me to keep in touch with myself. I also designed course materials, wrote plays in English and French (I have a French mother and close ties with France). I moved to Kent in 1996 and joined The Poetry School in 1997. I have two novels maturing in the loft, my fiction and reviews have been published in *Quality Women's Fiction* and poetry in *Staple New Writing*.'

JENNY HAMLETT lives in Cornwall. 'I began writing when in psychotherapy thirteen years ago. I was thirty-eight. I'd never met any writers and thought I was not clever enough to create a poem. I've never looked back. I now have an MA in creative writing, two children's stories published and poems in a variety of magazines and anthologies. I have also read my work on local radio and written garden poems for an exhibition. I now work as a creative writing teacher for Link into Learning (adult basic education) hoping that I can share with others some of the confidence that writing has given me.'

PAULINE HAWKESWORTH lives in Portsmouth. 'I came to the writing of poetry by default. I had wanted to be an artist but lack of family funds and fear on mother's part of me becoming "bohemian" led to leaving school at fifteen and working in an estate agents office. Soon after, whilst travelling home by bus, I was converted to words by a stream of metaphorical trees attacking me while I day-dreamed. Poetry became addictive. Family and its carapace has clung tightly. It's still difficult to find enough time, but gradually I am lifting up the shell and taking a new interest in the performance of my work.' Her collection of fifty-two poems, *Dust and Dew*, was published by Mitre Press in 1969. Twenty-nine years later she won a Redbeck Press competition and the resulting pamphlet was *Developing Green Films*.

PHOEBE HESKETH lives in Heath Charnock in Lancashire. The daughter of the pioneer radiologist A. E. Rayner, she was born in Preston in 1909 and educated at Cheltenham Ladies' College. During WW2 she worked for the *Bolton Evening News* and was later a freelance lecturer, poetry teacher and journalist, also producing scripts for the BBC. She began writing poetry at an early age but her first book was not published until 1939. It was followed by eleven further books before her New and Collected Poems, *Netting the Sun* were published by Enitharmon in 1989. Her poetry for younger readers has been published in *Song of Sunlight* (1974) and *Six of the Best* (Puffin, 1989). Her most recent collection is *A Box of Silver Birch* (Enitharmon, 1997).

NORAH HILL lives in Middlesbrough. 'I was born in 1945. I began story-making – "telling aloud" – when a baby before I could write. My first job was a pickle-onion pricer and my current one is as a poet working in a day-centre for the disabled. My first male critic (a Teddy Boy in a M'bro Coffee Bar) was unhelpful – he thought my poem "Prometheus" was "about matches". I failed O-level GCE Eng. Lit. twice and was fired from a Department Store for inability to grasp the complexities of the re-fund kiosk – but I have gained generous awards from Northern Arts and the Society of Authors to write my own books.' Her first poem was published in *PN Review* (1980), first solo poetry book, *Over the Border* (Mudfog, 1998). Her book of stories is *Of Many-Coloured Glass* (Paranoia Press, 1992).

LIZ HOUGHTON lives in London. 'My writing focusses on the fine detail of relationships – between the generations, between siblings, and between the sexes. I was born in 1945. I have a degree in Social Sciences from Birmingham University and studied English Literature at Sydney University. I worked in journalism for twenty-seven years, mainly on national newspapers. Six years ago I gave up to concentrate on creative writing, poetry and novels.' Her poetry has appeared in a variety of magazines and anthologies, including *The Long Pale Corridor, Contemporary Poems of Bereavement* (Bloodaxe, 1996).

SUE HUBBARD lives in London and is the founder member of Blue Nose Poets which runs workshops and events in London and residential courses at the Abbey in Sutton Courtney, Oxford. 'As a single mother of three small children running my own antique business, I did not start writing seriously until my late thirties. I have now transmuted into an art critic who has written regularly for the *New Statesman* and *Time Out*, broadcaster, novelist, award-winning poet and Arvon Tutor. I held the Poetry Society's first-ever Residency as Public Art Poet and my IMAX poem at Waterloo is London's largest public poem.' Her first collection, *Everything Begins with the Skin* was published by Enitharmon Press in 1994 and her first novel *Depth of Field* by Dewi Lewis Publishing in 2000. She is included in the anthology, *Oxford Poets 2000*, from Carcanet.

NICKI JACKOWSKA lives in East Sussex. She has published six collections of poetry – the latest, *Lighting a Slow Fuse, New and Selected Poems* (Enitharmon, 1998) – three novels and a book on language/creative writing, *Write for Life*. She has received an Arts Council Award for fiction and an American foundation award to write her fourth novel. She is working on a new collection, *Spikenard*. 'I have worked as a professional writer and tutor all my life, drawing on rural and urban landscapes for inspiration. My work is born of contrasts and excavations, the experience of working in Cornwall, Languedoc, Yorkshire, Lancashire and now Brighton. I am currently preparing *Jung and Lost Worlds*, a work drawing on a lifelong interest in the relationship between analysis and the creative process.'

BARBARA JAGGER now lives in Derbyshire 'closer to grandchildren, the moors and family roots'. 'Cambridge graduate, single parent, with a career in social work, I made time for writing by early retirement. I wrote my first report on myself and won a national life story award. It is in poetry that I have found most creative energy – and it's largely from women of a certain age that I find understanding and critical comment for my work. Working on "Elderstory", a S. Warwickshire mental health project, I have been scribe to older people with dementia, helping them tell their story and writing poems about this process. The closeness to another's identity, and the fear of loss of identity in Alzheimer's, seems central to the poetry task.' Birdsedge Press published her *Slow Cows* (1998). *Peach Leaf Curl* follows.

MARIA JASTRZEBSKA lives in Brighton, Sussex. 'I was born in Poland in 1953 and came to London as a small child. I am the author of *Postcards From Poland and other correspondences* with artist Jola Scicinska (Working Press, 1991). I was one of the editors of *Forum Polek*, the Polish Women's Forum, a bi-lingual anthology. As for late-starting? Yes! I am making up now for time lost through illness and also to that self-doubt which rattles many a good woman.' Her work appears in various other anthologies, most recently *Knowing ME: Women Speak about Myalgic Encephalomyelitis and Chronic Fatigue Syndrome* (The Women's Press, 1997) and *Not For The Academy; Lesbian Poets* (Onlywomen Press, 1999).

ELIZABETH JENNINGS was born in Lincolnshire in 1926 and now lives in Oxford. She has had seventeen collections of poetry published, beginning in 1953 with *Poems*. Her choice from these was included in *Collected Poems*, published by Carcanet in 1986. This includes translations and poems for children. In the Preface to *Collected Poems* she says, 'Art is not self-expression, while, for me, "confessional poetry" is almost a contradiction in terms.' Anne Stevenson has written of her work, 'Hers is a rare, enlightened, classical – and extremely tough – sensibility . . . *Collected Poems* not only represents Elizabeth Jennings at her best, but contains some of the finest lyric poetry of the 20th century.'

MARTHA KAPOS is an American living in London. 'After a degree in classics at Harvard, I came to London to study painting and the history of art at the Chelsea College of Art where I now teach. Reading, particularly contemporary American poets and French symbolist poets, had been very important to me before I even dreamt of writing myself. About ten years ago, finding myself at a particularly significant point of convergence of circumstances, emotional and practical, I started writing, and since then poetry has become the focus of my life. In 1989, the Many Press brought out a pamphlet and poems have been published in a number of magazines, including *Agenda, Rialto, Poetry London, Thumbscrew* and the *TLS*.'

ELIZABETH KAY lives in Surrey. 'I was born in 1949 of Polish/ English parentage, studied fine art, and now divide my time between writing, illustration and teaching. I have had radio plays broadcast and short stories published (one televised) and a novel recently, but only had the confidence to try poetry after completing a Creative Writing MA in my forties. My first solo undertaking is *The Spirit Collection*, published by Manifold. My poetry has appeared in magazines and I am a regular contributor to *Manifold*. I won the Cardiff International Competition in 1999 with a rhyming sestina "Pond Life".'

JACKIE KAY lives in Manchester. She is poet, playwright, novelist. Her first poetry collection, *The Adoption Papers* (Bloodaxe, 1991), tells the story, her story, of a black girl adopted by a white Scottish couple. It received a Scottish Arts Council Book Award, a Saltire Book of the Year Award and a Forward Prize. She won the Signal Poetry Award for *Two's Company* (Blackie, 1992), her book of poems for children, and a Somerset Maugham Award for her second collection, *Other Lovers* (Bloodaxe, 1993). *Off-Colour*, her third collection, was published by Bloodaxe in 1998. Fleur Adcock has written of 'Warm, tough, painful and often very funny poems'. Her first novel, *Trumpet*, was published by Picador. Her poems were incorporated in a feature-film shown on BBC 2 and have been broadcast on Radio 4.

JUDITH KAZANTZIS lives in London. 'Being a woman has certainly delayed but also perhaps been the wellhead of my poetry. It was only after my children were at school, by 1973, that I found both the energy and also something real to say as a poet, namely the exploration of myself as a woman stuck in traditional roles, my life like beer gone sadly flat. It was of course Plath's genius that started me off again. Encouraged by the women's movement, I promised myself that in whatever I wrote I would value women.' *Minefield* was published in 1977. Recent books are: *Swimming Through the Grand Hotel* (Enitharmon, 1997), *The Odysseus Poems, Fictions on the Odyssey of Homer* (Cargo Press, 1999), with a related piece for two voices, *Sex, Lies and Odysseus*.

MIMI KHALVATI lives in London working as a free-lance creative writing tutor and Coordinator of The Poetry School which she founded. She started writing in her early forties after attending an Arvon Foundation course. She has published three full collections with Carcanet, *In White Ink* (1991), *Mirrorwork* (1995), for which she received an Arts Council of England Writer's Award and *Entries on Light* (1997). Her *Selected Poems* was published by Carcanet in 2000.

LOTTE KRAMER lives in Peterborough. 'I was born in Mainz, Germany and came to England as a refugee child in 1939, undertaking all kinds of work (laundry, dress-shop) while studying Art and History of Art. After being transplanted from London to the country, I began writing late, facing up to childhood memories and loss. I felt isolated and writing released trauma. My last collection, *Selected and New Poems 1980-1997* (Rockingham Press, 1997), includes work from six previous collections. In 1999, a bilingual edition of selected poems was published in Germany: *Heimweh / Homesick* (Brandes and Apsel, Frankfurt am Main). A new collection, *The Phantom Lane* is due from Rockingham Press in November 2000.'

STEVIE KRAYER lives in Wales, in Lampeter. 'One morning at primary school, our teacher read us "Adelstrop" – that was my poetic annunciation. At sixteen I chucked away a thick folder of poems. The odd one forced its way through at university, while I brought up a family and pursued various inappropriate careers. In my forties I began writing more and more, and to give more time to write my partner and I moved to rural West Wales. My first published book was a translation of Rilke's *Das Stündenbuch* and the second a collection of my own poetry, *Voices from a Burning Boat* (Salzburg University Press). Apart from causing a quarter-century of paralysing self-deprecation, being a woman has not played more part in my writing than has being Jewish, left-wing, the granddaughter of immigrants, the wife of a Welshman and a Quaker.'

PHILIPPA LAWRENCE lives in Salisbury where she founded Kick Start Poets. 'Traditionally, an appalling childhood produces writers but you become a natural victim whose house is built on sand, always an Outsider. Violins! I studied Dress, Set and Costume Design and Stage Management and I pioneered restoring textiles in stately homes, creating conservation centres at Knole, Hatfield and Castle Howard and designing innovative equipment. Losing my voice in 1989 and reciting poetry as therapy made me start writing again, taking Arvon and other courses. My poems have been published in the *Evening Standard, Western Daily Press, Literary Review, Spectator* and *South* (Southern Counties' biannual poetry magazine for which I selected their October 1999 poems on behalf of Wiltshire). I am on the Council of the Society of Women Writers and Journalists.'

DINAH LIVINGSTONE lives in London. Her most recent collections of poetry are: *Time on Earth: Selected and New Poems* (Rockingham Press, 1999), *May Day* (Katabasis, 1997) and *Second Sight* (Katabasis, 1993). She ran the Camden Voices poetry group from 1978-1998 and her *Poetry Handbook for Readers and Writers* (Macmillan, 1992) is dedicated to them. Her translations include: *Prayer in the National Stadium* by María Eugenia Bravo Calderara (1992), *Poets of the Nicaraguan Revolution* (1993), *Life for Each* by Daisy Zamora (1994), all from Katabasis, and *Nosotras: Poems by Nicaraguan Women* (NSC, 1999). A prose book, *The Poetry of Earth* is due in 2000.

SUE MACINTYRE lives in London. 'I have been writing poetry in an occasional way for a long time but it has become much more centre stage and absorbing recently, now that I am winding down my working life and my children are grown up. Writing workshops have been very important in this process and my first publication has been in workshop anthologies. I am currently working on a sequence drawing on my father's letters from 1911-18 and 1939-40. "Letters from the Concertina File" is one of these poems.'

BARBARA MARSH lives in London. 'I'm a singer/song-writer/musician, so music and especially words have always had a strong pull on me. It has only been in the last year that my poetry has felt "right" to me as if some sudden shift has occurred. I am an American and have lived in London for over sixteen years and I think that cross-cultural reference adds an angle to my work.'

GERDA MAYER, who now lives in Chingford, was born in Karlsbad, Czechoslovakia and came to England in 1939 at the age of eleven. Among her collections are a shared collection with Elon and Halpern, *Treble Poets 2* and *The Knockabout Show*, both from Chatto and Windus; *Monkey on the Analyst's Couch* (Ceolfrith Press), which was a Poetry Book Society Recommendation; and *A Heartache of Grass* (Peterloo Poets). Her latest book is *Bernini's Cat* (Iron Press, 1999).

JOAN MICHELSON lives in London and works as Associate Senior Lecturer at the University of Wolverhampton, responsible for Creative Writing and Holocaust Studies: Literature. 'I recently returned to poetry after a long period of concentration on prose and am working on a collection, *The Eternal Lesson*, treating the journey through grief.' Her work has been published in *British Council New Writing 3 and 4*; also in magazines in the UK and USA, including *Stand, London Magazine, Writing Women, Spare Rib*, the *Jewish Quarterly*, the *Alaska Quarterly*, the *Kansas Quarterly* and the *Antioch Review*. Fellowships for writing residencies have been awarded by the Ragdale Foundation, Illinois (1998) and the Virginia Centre for the Creative Arts and she has won several prizes in poetry competitions.

SUSAN MICHIE lives in London. 'I come from a family of Scottish painters. After leaving school I went straight into the film industry and worked in the cutting-room on such films as *If . . .* directed by Lindsay Anderson and *Deliverance* directed by John Boorman. I began writing poetry five years ago after a brief period of Jungian analysis. The attempt to combine words and images, in any medium, is a continuing source of interest.'

ELMA MITCHELL was born in Airdrie, Scotland in 1919 and now lives in Somerset where she works as a free-lance writer and translator. She is a professional librarian and has worked in broadcasting, publishing and journalism in London. Four poetry collections have been published by Peterloo Poets: *The Poor Man in the Flesh* (1976), *The Human Cage* (1979), *Furnished Rooms* (1983), and *People Etcetera* (1987), which included the best poems from the two earliest collections (now out-of-print) and new poems. She was first prize winner in the Cheltenham Festival Poetry Competition in 1977.

LYN MOIR lives in Southampton. 'I was born in Glasgow in 1934 and wrote early, encouraged by my parents, getting published in the US when living there 1949-52. Intense disapproval from my husband about writing meant that I closed down for twenty-five years. After his death I felt able to write again – unable to stop. I have now been published in fifteen magazines: the most important things in my life now are writing and the friends it has brought me.'

FELICITY NAPIER lives in Twickenham where she teaches writing groups in mental health settings. 'I have been writing poetry, short fiction and drama for twenty years, poetry remaining my first love. My poems have won prizes and have appeared in numerous magazines and anthologies and been broadcast on radio and TV. A selection of my work appeared in *Anvil New Poets* (1990). The writing process is an integral part of my life, my touchstone and survival route.'

CAROLINE NATZLER lives in London where she works part-time as a lawyer for a local authority and also runs creative writing workshops at City University, Goldsmiths College and City Lit. 'Writing has always been important to me. The impulse has shifted from a young desire to voice my inner self and a sense that the world needed to be written, to a commitment to writing as a lesbian, and latterly to a pleasure in the craft . . . Although I wrote poetry in my teens I came to think of it as too difficult or esoteric and did not start again until I was forty when a friend suggested that a change of form from short stories might help me through writer's block. Which it did.' Her short-story collection is *Water Wings* (Onlywomen Press, 1990), poetry collection, *Speaking the Wetlands* (Pikestaff Press, 1998).

HELENA NELSON (the poet's pen-name) lives in Scotland. 'I have always written poetry as a slightly eccentric secret habit. I have always read it too and at difficult times specific poems were very important to me and have even kept me going. I only started to write for publication when, at forty, I separated from my husband. I wanted readers. I wanted to write poems that would matter to other people in the way others' poems had mattered to me. I found it more difficult than I expected. Everywhere was advice for "new" poets. I am not "new" but in my mid-forties and still trying.'

EILÉAN NÍ CHUILLEANÁIN lives in Southern Ireland where she is Head of the Department of English at Trinity College, Dublin. She was born in 1942. Her latest collection is *The Brazen Serpent* (Gallery Books, 1994).

GRACE NICHOLS now lives in Sussex. She was born in 1950 and grew up in Guyana, working there as a journalist and reporter. She came to England in 1977 and has published children's books and three collections of poetry – *i is a long-memoried woman* (Virago, 1983) won the Commonwealth Poetry Prize. Virago has also published *The Fat Black Woman's Poems* (1984), *Lazy Thoughts of a Lazy Woman* (1989), and *Sunris* (1996). They also published her novel, *Whole of a Morning* (1986).

DOROTHY NIMMO lives in Settle, North Yorkshire. 'I was born in 1932, educated at York and Cambridge and spent thirty years being a wife-and-mother, a gardener and a goat-herd. I started writing in the 1980s in a WEA class, and went on to Arvon courses and an MA in creative writing at Lancaster University, 1989. I left home to be caretaker of the Friends Meeting House in Gloucester and am now caretaker at the Settle FMH. I have had four books of poems published, the latest, *The Children's Game* (Smith/Doorstop Books, 1998), was a Poetry Book Society Recommendation. I won a Cholmondeley Award in 1997.'

BARBARA NOEL-SCOTT lives in Cambridge. 'I have written verse from childhood. Marriage, the War years, bringing up four children occupied me until I was nearly fifty. I began writing more ambitiously in the early 1960s. The first of four booklets was published by Outposts in 1962. I won two poetry prizes and was asked to read my poems at the then venue of the Poetry Society, Earls Court Square. I continued to be accepted for poetry magazines and anthologies, including the Femina Collection of Women's Poetry, *Without Adam* (1968). Three more collections followed, the last *Seasons and Celebrations* (Envoi Poets, 1993).

EAMER O'KEEFFE is an Irish woman living in London. 'I wrote my first poem at seven but it took forty-five years to find myself as a poet. Now I write to make sense of things, and to share that with others – something I do more easily in England than in my native Ireland. I was a war baby and in many ways I've experienced war for most of my life. Over the past seven years, I've been a performer with Survivors Poetry, and have been widely published in magazines and anthologies. In 1999, I co-edited with Lisa Boardman, *Fresher than Green, Brighter than Orange*, an anthology of poetry by Irishwomen living in London, published by Survivors Poetry. It includes my poem "Chords". My most recent publication is *War Chronicle*, a long poem set in 1938 and 1939 – my contribution to the old and new millennia.'

JENNIE OSBORNE lives in Totnes, Devon. 'I started to write again in my late thirties after a gap of many years, having left a career as a librarian in London to establish a business in Cornwall. As a late-starter, I have much appreciated the constructive support and encouragement of other writers, both through workshopping and personal contact.' Her poems have been published in a variety of magazines. She is a member of Liskeard Poets and of Second Light network of women poets.

EVANGELINE PATERSON sadly died while this anthology was in preparation. In the last part of her life she lived in Jesmond, Newcastle on Tyne. 'I started to write in the 1970s when my children were past the dependent stage. I expect I write more about domestic affairs than a man would, and I think I deal with them from a more personal perspective.' She was a joint editor of *Other Poetry* for many years. Her final collection was *A Game of Soldiers* (Stride, 1997).

PASCALE PETIT lives in London, working as a creative writing tutor and poetry editor of *Poetry London*. 'I was born in Paris in 1953 and trained as a sculptor at the Royal College of Art. I have always written poetry but it took me a long time to develop because I was mainly a sculptor. At that time it was much harder for women to get published, especially if the subject matter was emotional. When I stopped being a visual artist I applied myself wholeheartedly to poetry. The page became my studio where I had to create my world and make it real. Metaphors and images replaced materials. The labour-intensive process of sculpture I now apply to making my poems.' Her first collection, *Heart of a Deer* (1998), was published by Enitharmon who will also bring out *The Zoo Father*. A pamphlet, *Icefall Climbing,* was published by Smith/Doorstop in 1994.

PATRICIA POGSON lives near Kendal in Cumbria. 'I began writing in my early thirties when my children started school. I was encouraged by early publication and have since produced five collections. The latest, *The Tides in the Basin* was published by Flambard Press in 1994 and I am at work on another.'

CAROLINE PRICE lives in Tunbridge Wells, Kent, where she works as a violinist and teacher. 'I started writing prose as a child and added poetry in my twenties. Writing for me lives hand in hand with music and has always been an essential and unquestioned part of my life. "Night Fishing" is from my second collection, *Pictures Against Skin* (Rockingham Press, 1994). I have given readings in various venues including the South Bank, and in 1997 was one of ten poets involved in a women writers' exchange, taking part in readings and discussions in England and Northern Europe.'

PAULINE PRIOR-PITT lives in North Uist in the Outer Hebrides. 'As I approached forty, I began to write poetry in an attempt to prevent insanity from toppling my juggling act as wife, mother with three teenagers, also lecturer . . . I write humorously and seriously about how women cope with men, with children, the domestic scene, buying clothes, gynaecology, politics, ageing and of course love and death. I have performed my poems at Literature Festivals, on BBC Radio 4, on television. I regularly entertain "ladies who lunch" with my one-woman show.' Her first book, *Waiting Women* (Spike Press, 1989) has been reprinted seven times with a revised edition, foreword by Maureen Lipman, July 1999. Her other collections, both from Spike Press, are *Still Standing in a Plant Pot* (1994) and *Addresses and Dreams* (1997).

ALISON PRYDE lives near Berwick on Tweed. 'Thirty-four years ago, after a decade or so living abroad, I returned to my family farm and childhood home in Northumberland. I have written for nine years: my first collection, *Have We had Easter Yet?* (Peterloo Poets, 1998), was published when I was sixty. The title poem, about my mother who had Alzheimer's, won second prize in the 1994 Peterloo competition. My poems are fairly wide-ranging, but I always return to writing about life in a relatively isolated rural community, about my experience of growing up as an only child and about bringing up my children in the same house (where I now live alone). I obviously write from a feminine viewpoint but I do not see that as especially significant. Writing is part of the life I lead and thus is woven into it.'

LESLEY QUAYLE lives on a farm just outside Leeds. 'I have always written poetry but after the birth of my children I shelved my ambitions for eighteen years. I began writing again when I was forty and it was as if somebody had pulled a cork from a bottle. Work was accepted fairly early on and I was a winner in the BBC Wildlife Magazine Poet of the Year Competition. Now I try to be as committed as possible to poetry. I give readings, co-edit *Aireings* poetry magazine and go into local primary schools working on children's poetry. My first collection *A Perfect Spit at the Stars* (Spanna in the Works) came out in 1999. Being a "late starter" and a woman I have to work hard on my confidence as well as my poetry, still performing juggling acts to make room for writing.'

NICKY RICE sadly died during the preparation of this anthology. She was then living in Brighton. She was born near Killarney, Ireland. She read English at University College, London and after raising a family of three children she became a teacher, then a free-lance writer. She won the National Poetry Competition in 1990. Her poems have appeared in many newspapers and journals, including *Cumberland Review* (USA), *London Magazine*, *The Observer*, *Poetry Review* and *Writing Women* and she also read on radio and television. Her collection, *Coming Up to Midnight*, was published by Enitharmon in 1994.

DAPHNE ROCK lives in London. '"Changing" is the first poem I had published. I was fifty-seven. It was written during an Arvon course with Liz Lochhead where I learned a good deal and found I could call myself a poet. Bringing up children, getting educated, then teaching and working with teenagers in trouble – it took all this to build confidence in myself, to be brave enough to take writing out of the bottom desk drawer and chance it with the critics. Even now I lack the ruthless self-interest of the really dedicated writer. If it came to a choice, the children would come first but one of the advantages of a late start is that this is not likely to be demanded. My life is my life and I will not regard the earlier years as wasted.' Her collection, *Waiting for Trumpets* was published by Peterloo Poets in 1998.

VERONICA ROSPIGLIOSI sadly died while this anthology was in preparation, a short time after the publication of her first poetry pamphlet, *Reckitt's Blue* (Hearing Eye, 1999). She was born in Yorkshire in 1937 and began writing seriously in the early 1990s. She was a regular attender at London workshops and credited these with the gradual emergence of finished work in her own voice.

CAROL RUMENS lives in London. 'I have published ten collections of poems, the most recent *Holding Pattern* (Blackstaff, 1998). Being a woman writer has probably made it easier to get published but not easier to be taken seriously.'

FRANCES SACKETT was born in 1948 in Wales and now lives in Stockport. 'I began to write poetry in my teens but it was not until my daughters were growing up and I returned to study that the poetry returned. This was influenced by the range of American, Russian, Old English and Modern English writers that my degree covered, but also by the landscape of rural Wales that I had grown up in. I have always felt an empathy towards the struggling artist as well as the writer – the art of Gwen John and the women travel writers through the centuries have been a powerful example of excellence against the odds.' Her first collection is *The Hand Glass* (Seren, 1996).

207

CAROLE SATYAMURTI lives and works in London as poet and sociologist, teaching at the University of East London and at the Tavistock Clinic. 'I am principally interested in the relevance of psychoanalytic ideas to the stories people tell about themselves, whether in formal autobiography or in everyday encounters.' She won the National Poetry Competition in 1986 and was awarded an Arts Council Writers' Award in 1988. She has published *Broken Moon* (1987), *Changing the Subject* (1990), *Striking Distance* (1994), all from OUP, together with *Selected Poems* (1998). *Love and Variations* was issued by Bloodaxe in 2000. She has given many readings and is an experienced workshop tutor; with Gregory Warren Wilson she recently conducted a series of workshops on Art and Poetry at the National Gallery.

MYRA SCHNEIDER lives in London. 'Writing has been essential to my well-being since I was nine. In the early 1960s after I'd left university I found the poetry scene unsympathetic, so for years I concentrated on writing prose and I had novels published for children and teenagers. In my forties I started writing poetry again and it slowly dawned on me that this was the medium in which I expressed myself best. I write to explore my own life and the lives of others. I love using narrative in poetry. Perhaps the keynote of my work is finding a voice. My most recent collections are *The Panic Bird* and *Insisting on Yellow: New and Selected Poems*, both Enitharmon Press (1998 and 2000).' Her writing handbook written with poet John Killick, *Writing for Self-Discovery* was published by Element Books (1998).

RUTH SHARMAN lives in London. 'My first collection, *Birth of the Owl Butterflies* (Picador, 1997), was published in the year that our first child was born. I had come late to motherhood and it had taken ten years for the book of poems to mature. At six I was uprooted from Southern India and removed to a place where what mattered was tying my shoelaces and telling the time. The sense of dislocation continued – I wore academic achievements as a kind of mask and dis-connection from my inner world led to constant illness. My mother died just as I was finishing a Ph.D. at Cambridge and it was then through writing and psychoanalysis that I began to obtain a sense of identity. For me, poetry comes out of an intense preoccupation with time passing. It is through poetry that I feel most intensely alive.'

HYLDA SIMS divides her time between Ipswich and London. She has had poems published in magazines and anthologies. Her narrative sequence, 'Reaching Peckham' has been set to music and performed at the Dulwich Festival and on the fringe. Her novel, *Inspecting the Island*, is published by Seven-ply Yarns. She has a long-standing involvement in folk music and jazz. 'Writing more conscientiously later in life must be a substitute for not singing for a living any more!'

RUTH SMITH lives in Bromley in Kent. 'I've written poetry for four years and found nothing to equal the excitement. Having spent a career as an English teacher passing judgment on children's writing I began to appreciate the difficul-ties and admire their talent. I had read little contemporary poetry and, after first managing my writing on my own with many failures and a few poems published, I found that a poetry workshop at Morley College helped tremendously.' She won the London Writers' Prize in 1996 and two of her poems appeared in the first edition of Faber and Faber's *First Pressings*.

MARGARET SPEAK lives in York. 'I began writing in my late thirties in response to the death of my younger sister. I was encouraged by early success in competitions and being a featured poet in Giant Steps. Since then I've also had prizes with short stories and gained a Master's degree in writing. Exploring ideas and images in words helps me make sense of emotional experience and allows me to re-tell stories which reflect women's issues through changing social conditions.' She has a collection, *The Firefly Cage* (Redbeck Press, 1998).

ANNE STEVENSON is an American poet long resident in Britain. She has had ten collections of poetry published by the Oxford University Press. After the collapse of OUP Poetry in 1998 she contracted with Bloodaxe Books: *Granny Scarecrow* appeared in May 2000.

BREDA SULLIVAN lives in Co. Westmeath, Republic of Ireland. 'I have led a very busy life being a full-time primary school teacher for over thirty years, raising four children and caring for my husband and home. I began writing in my early forties and was fortunate to have poems published in journals and after five years my first collection, *A Smell of Camphor* published by Salmon Publishing, who had the courage to give that initial break to many Irish women poets. Writing is as necessary to me as breathing and there is no feeling to compare with the elation when I finish a poem.' Her most recent collection *After the Ball* was published by Salmon in 1998.

ISOBEL THRILLING lives in Romford in Essex. She was born in Suffolk, raised in a mining village in Yorkshire, went to Hull University and for many years was Head of an English Language Service in London. 'I first started writing after eye-operations which saved my sight. My work is very visual and perhaps, subconsciously, I am creating aural images. Poetry has made me aware of childhood traumas, which previously I had no way to express. I explore silences and what lies behind appearance. Women bring a different focus to words. Poetry is the writer's ectoplasm, a precipitation of the imagination, a leap across the synapses of the brain.' Her latest collection is *Spectrum Shift* from Littlewood (1991) and a new collection, *The Chemistry of Angels* is due from the Hull-based 'halfacrown press'.

SUSAN UTTING lives in Wokingham and works at Reading University as a creative writing tutor and in the editorial office of the Psychology Department. She organises events for Reading's Poets' Café and the performance group, Late Shift. 'Very much a late-starter, I failed the 11+, then left it to my forties to gain a first-class honours degree and to begin writing poetry. Now my poems are much anthologised and I was shortlisted for the Arvon prize in 1998.' Her first collection was *Scratched Initials* (Corridor Press, Reading, 1997); latest, *Something Small is Missing* (Smith/Doorstop Books, 1999: Poetry Business prize winner).

JOAN WADDLETON lives on the Isle of Wight. 'A career in further/ higher education involved me in a fair amount of writing but allowed me no room for poetry – published material was restricted to articles. Chairing the Isle of Wight Poetry Society for some years left me even less space! Having now retired, writing has surged to the forefront – no collection as yet, still at the stage of being "over the moon" if single poems are accepted by quality magazines. But writing and learning about writing are major sources of joy.'

SUSAN WICKS lives in Kent. 'I've almost always written but I didn't manage to get a book accepted until my early forties. Since then I've published six. The most recent book of poems is *The Clever Daughter* (Faber, 1996). For me the most telling difficulty was lack of self-confidence – what Americans call "the lack of a sense of entitlement". There were few models. I'm from a relatively unbookish background. The poetry met at school offered no way in – too soon then for me to have heard of Plath and Hughes. I wrote prose fiction in my teens and late twenties – it didn't occur to me that poetry was something a woman might write. These days I'm very aware of the many strong voices. In moments of discouragement I go back to Alicia Surkin Ostriker's Introduction to *Stealing the Language*; the case she quietly builds seems to me overwhelming.'

MERRYN WILLIAMS lives in Wootton, in Bedfordshire. 'I gave up writing poems at university and only took it up again when my younger children started at school.' Her latest collection of poems is *The Latin Master's Story* (Rockingham Press, 2000). She is editor of *The Interpreter's House* poetry magazine and edits for the Wilfred Owen Association.

PALORINE WILLIAMS lives in Sheffield where she runs a creative writing workshop for black women writers.

FRANCES WILSON lives in Ware, Hertfordshire. 'Writing has always shared space in my working life with teaching and illustrating. I wrote short stories until 1986 when I started writing poems. I have won prizes in various competitions. My pamphlet, *Where the Light Gets In* was published by Poet and Printer (1992) and my collection, *Close to Home* by Rockingham in 1993.'

DILYS WOOD lives in Dulwich, London. 'I wrote when a school-girl in South Wales, singing as I walked. Reading English at Cambridge in the 1960s had the effect of killing my writing – a strange effect, not an uncommon one. I found the contemporary idiom apparently unrelated to the great tradition – and failed to access the good stuff. Thirty years later I caught up with the essential half-dozen twentieth-century English and Irish poets, the Russians, Rilke and Celan, the battery of early and mid-century American genius. In the 1990s, I found a more varied, interesting, accessible poetry scene. I made contacts among women poets, founding the Second Light Network.' Her collection is *Women Come to a Death* (Katabasis, 1997).

LYNNE WYCHERLEY lives in Kidlington, Oxfordshire. 'Born in 1962, I began writing in 1996 and was a Blue Nose Poet of the Year in 1998. I have worked in nature conservation and have won an award for rural poetry. I do not regret being a late starter – I'm glad to have seen different aspects of life, love, grief before beginning writing.' Her pamphlet collection, *Cracks in the Ice* is published by Acumen.

PAM ZINNEMANN-HOPE lives in Toller Porcorum, Dorset. 'I was born in Leeds. In my twenties I wrote and performed poetry and published, including *Ichibu, Fragments of Childhood* with Outposts. When I had my children, writing poetry became impossible. In 1986–7, Walker published my "Ned" books for children. I then trained and worked as a counsellor. My poetry came back to life when my eldest daughter left home. Through a sequence of poems (some have appeared in magazines) I am exploring the sense of dislocation and fragmentation within my family caused by events in Europe in the mid-twentieth century. My parents eloped from Germany to Russia and were imprisoned in the Stalin purges. Though they rarely spoke about the past, they have left a complex emotional legacy.'

Acknowledgements

The editors and Enitharmon Press would like to express their thanks to the following publishers for permission to reprint poems:

ACUMEN
Lynne Wycherley, 'Earth Man', *Cracks in the Ice*, Acumen Pamphlet, 1999

ARC
Jacqueline Brown, 'In the Room 1', *Thinking Egg*, 1998

BLACKWATER PRESS
Catherine Byron, 'Minding You', *The White Page, An Bilfogbhan*, jointly published with Salmon, 1999
Kate Foley, 'Matching Flowers', *A Year Without Apricots*, 1999

BLOODAXE
Moniza Alvi, 'Throwing Out My Father's Dictionary', *Carrying My Wife*, 2000
Elizabeth Bartlett, 'God Is Dead, Nietzsche' and 'Smile for Daddy', *Two Women Dancing, New and Selected Poems*, 1995
Pamela Gillilan, 'The Mistress', 'Looking North', *All-Steel Traveller*, 1994
Jackie Kay, 'The Telling Part', *The Adoption Papers*, 1991
Carole Rumens, 'Before the Wars', *Thinking of Skin, New and Selected Poems*, 1993

CAMPION
Suzanne Burrows, 'A Time of Cherries', *The Dream Garden and Other Poems*, 1998

CARCANET
Gillian Clarke, 'Migraine', *Five Fields*, 1999
Anne Cluysenaar, 'The Knife', *Time Slips*, 1997
Jean Earle, 'At the South Pole', *A Trial of Strength*, 1980
Elaine Feinstein, 'Dad', *Selected Poems*, 1994
Elizabeth Jennings, 'One Flesh', *Collected Poems*, 1986
Mimi Khalvati, 'Baba Mostafa', *In White Ink*, 1991, 'Coma', *Mirrorwork*, 1995, 'Knocking on the Door', *Entries on Light*, 1997

CULVERHAY PRESS
R. V. Bailey, 'Father's Things', *Course Work*, 1997

DUCKWORTH
Gladys Mary Coles, 'Ithica-Liverpool', *Leafburners: New and Selected Poems*, 1986

ENITHARMON
Hilary Davies, 'Beachy Head', *The Shanghai Owner of the Bonsai Shop*, 1991
Phoebe Hesketh, 'Dilemma', *The Leave Train*, 1994

Sue Hubbard, 'Letter', *Everything Begins with the Skin*, 1994
Nicki Jackowska, 'The Woman who Mistook her Father for an Irishman',
Lighting a Slow Fuse, New and Selected Poems, 1998
Judith Kazantzis, 'Dada', *Swimming through the Grand Hotel*, 1997
Pascale Petit, 'My Mother's Clothes', *Heart of a Deer*, 1998
Nicky Rice, 'Mother's Room', *Coming Up to Midnight*, 1994
Myra Schneider, 'The Photograph', *The Panic Bird*, 1998, 'Soup and Slavery',
Insisting on Yellow, New and Selected Poems, 2000

FABER
Susan Wicks, 'Stilt-walker', *Singing Underwater*, 1992

FIVE LEAVES PUBLICATIONS
Liz Cashdan, 'Laughing All the Way', *Laughing All the Way*, 1995

FLAMBARD
Wanda Barford, 'Sorting Things Out', *A Moon at the Door*, 1999
Cynthia Fuller, 'My Father's Dreams', *Instructions for the Desert*, 1996
Judy Gahagan, 'The Colour of the Old Man's Eyes', *Crossing the Noman's Land*,
1999

GALLERY PRESS
Eiléan Ní Chuilleanáin, 'The Tale of Me', *The Brazen Serpent*, 1994

HALE AND IREMONGER
Katherine Gallagher, 'Distances', *Passengers to the City*, 1995

HEADLAND
Anna Adams, 'To My Mother', *Memorial Tree*, 1993

HEARING EYE
Veronica Rospigliosi, 'Leavetaking', *Reckitt's Blue*, Hearing Eye Pamphlet, 1999

HIPPOPOTAMUS PRESS
Lotte Kramer, 'Love Letters' and 'The Non-Emigrant', *The Desecration of Trees*,
1994

IRON PRESS
Gerda Mayer, 'Make Believe', *Bernini's Cat*, 1999

JACKSON'S ARM
Jill Bamber, 'Broken Necklace', *Altered States*, 1996

KATABASIS
Dinah Livingstone, 'Stepmother', *Prepositions and Conjunctions*, 1997

LITTLEWOOD
Isobel Thrilling, 'Mother', *Spectrum Shift*, 1991

MIDDAY
Anne Born, 'End of the Row', *Changing Views*, 1979

MUDFOG
Norah Hill, 'Dürer's Young Hare', *Over the Border*, 1998

NATIONAL POETRY FOUNDATION
Merryn Williams, 'Heading for the Heights', *The Sun's Yellow Eye*, 1997

ONLYWOMEN PRESS
Kate Foley, 'My Father, Counting Sheep', *Soft Engineering*, 1994

OVERSTEPS PRESS
Patricia Bishop, 'Woman Washing', *Saving Dragons*, 1999

OXFORD UNIVERSITY PRESS
Moniza Alvi, 'Throwing Out My Father's Dictionary', *The Country at My Shoulder*, 1993
Carole Satyamurti, 'Erdywurble', *Broken Moon*, 1987, 'Where Are You?', *Striking Distance*, 1994
Anne Stevenson, 'When the Camel is Dust it Goes Through the Needle's Eye', *Collected Poems, 1955–1995*, 1995

PETERLOO POETS
Anna Adams, 'To My Mother', *Nobodies*, 1990
U. A. Fanthorpe, 'Fanfare', *Standing To*, 1982
Elma Mitchell, 'Mother, Dear Mother', *People Etcetera*, 1987
Alison Pryde, 'I'll See You Down the Lane', *Have We Had Easter Yet?*, 1998
Daphne Rock, 'Changing', *Waiting for Trumpets*, 1998

PHAROS PRESS
Priscilla Borthwick, 'Forest', *Deep Waters*, 1996

PIKESTAFF PRESS
Caroline Natzler, 'There', *Speaking the Wetlands*, 1998

RACE TODAY PUBLICATIONS
Jean Binta Breeze, 'natural high', *Riddym Ravings*, 1988

REDBECK PRESS
Pauline Hawkesworth, 'Two Statues', *Developing Green Films*, 1998

RIVELIN PRESS
Patricia Pogson, 'Bo Tree', *Before the Roadshow*, 1983

ROCKINGHAM PRESS
Anne-Marie Fyfe, 'Upturn', *Late Crossing*, 1999
Lotte Kramer, 'On Shutting the Door', *The Shoemaker's Wife, Selected and New Poems*, 1997
Caroline Price, 'Night Fishing', *Pictures Against Skin*, 1994
Frances Wilson, 'Bathing My Mother', *Close to Home*, 1993

SALMON
Catherine Byron, 'Minding You', *The White Page, An Bilfogbhan*, Salmon with Blackwater, 1999

SALZBURG UNIVERSITY PRESS
Stevie Krayer, 'My Mother Dressed for the Wedding', *Voices from a Burning Boat*, 1997

SEREN
Frances Sackett, 'Another Kind of Skin', *The Hand Glass*, 1996

SHOESTRING PRESS
Nadine Brummer, 'That Rank Bed', *A Question of Blue Tulips*, 1999

SIDGWICK AND JACKSON
Judith Kazantzis, 'midwife', *Minefield*, 1987

SMITH/DOORSTOP
Katherine Frost, 'Winners', *The Sixth Channel*, 1995
Dorothy Nimmo, 'Exorcism' and 'My Father's Shadow', *The Children's Game*, 1998
Susan Utting, 'The Spoon Maker's Daughter', *Something Small is Missing*, 1999

SPANNA IN THE WORKS
Lesley Quayle, 'The Woman Who Drank Us Up', *A Perfect Spit at the Stars*, 1999

SPIKE PRESS
Pauline Prior-Pitt, 'Fitting', *Addresses and Dreams*, 1997

STRIDE
Evangeline Paterson, 'Griselda', *A Game of Soldiers*, 1997

VIRAGO
Grace Nichols, 'Praise Song for My Mother', *The Fat Black Woman's Poems*, 1984

WOMEN'S PRESS
Daphne Rock, 'Changing', *No Holds Barred*, 1985

WALDEAN PRESS
Gillie Bolton, 'Little Red Riding Hood and the Wolf', *Hole in the Moon*, 1997

We would also like to thank Devlin Barrett, literary executor, for permission to use 'Vigil' from his mother Blair Gibb's collection, *Tom's Diner*, published privately after her death

Poems also appeared in the following publications

AMBIT
Judith Kazantzis, 'My Dada', *Ambit* 134, 1993
Pascale Petit, 'Embrace of the Electric Eel', *Ambit* 160, 1999

Anvil New Poets Anthology 1990
Felicity Napier, 'I Do Not Want the Ceiling of the Sistine Chapel', 'I Have Taken the Suits and Shoes to Oxfam'

ARVON 1998 ANTHOLOGY, *The Ring of Words*
Anne-Marie Fyfe, 'Upturn'

BETE NOIR
Gillie Bolton, 'Little Red Riding Hood and the Wolf', Issue No. 10/11, Autumn 1990/Spring 1991

BIRMINGHAM AND MIDLAND INSTITUTE MAGAZINE / WILKINS INTERNATIONAL MEMORIAL PRIZE WINNERS
Elizabeth Kay, 'Phoenix'

BLOODAXE ANTHOLOGY, *New Women Poets* (ed. Carol Rumens), 1990
Jackie Kay, 'The Telling Part'

BLOODAXE ANTHOLOGY, *The Long Pale Corridor* (ed. Judi Benson & Agneta Falk), 1996
Liz Houghton, 'Caustic Soda'

BRASS BUTTERFLY #2, 1999
Moira Clark, 'Mushrooms'

BRITISH COUNCIL, *New Writing 3 Anthology 1994*
Caroline Price, 'Night Fishing'

CYPHERS
Lotte Kramer, 'Love Letters', 1989

ENCOUNTER
Gerda Mayer, 'Make Believe', 1998

ENVOI
Barbara Jagger, 'Anyway', *Envoi* 121, 1998
Lyn Moir, 'Handnotes', *Envoi* 122, 1999
Barbara Noel-Scott, 'Hansel and Gretel', *Envoi* 117, 1997

European Judaism, An Anthology (ed. Ruth Fainlight)
Wanda Barford, 'Sorting Things Out'

HEADLOCK
Pam Bridgeman, 'Cockatoo', *Headlock*, No. 9, October, 1999

THE INTERPRETER'S HOUSE
Sally Carr, 'Easter Outing', October 1999
Evangeline Paterson, 'Griselda', 1996
Joan Waddleton 'Fatherhood', 2000

Lancaster Literature Festival Anthology
Priscilla Borthwick, 'Out of Bounds', 1999
Frances Wilson, 'Bathing My Mother', 1990

LINES REVIEW
Catherine Byron, 'Shipping the Pictures from Belfast', 1996

Mutiny Poets, A HULL LITERARY FESTIVAL PUBLICATION
Carol Coiffait, 'The Last Apple'

THE OBSERVER
Lotte Kramer, 'The Non-Emigrant', 1990

OTHER POETRY
Jennie Osborne, 'The Naming of Flowers', 2000

OUTPOSTS
Patricia Pogson, 'Bo Tree', 1978

POETRY LONDON
Katherine Frost, 'Remission', Autumn 1997
Ruth Sharman, 'By Heart', Spring 1999

P. N. REVIEW
Anne Stevenson, 'Ariosto Dolente', Winter 1998–99

POETRY REVIEW
Nicki Jackowska, 'The Woman Who Mistook her Father for an Irishman',
Summer 1995

POETRY NOTTINGHAM INTERNATIONAL
Nicolette Golding, 'Wardrobes', Spring 1998
Margaret Speak, 'Ingredients of Glass'

POETRY WALES
Jane Duran, 'Spanish Peasant Boy', 1999
Anne Grimes, 'Alice's Cat, New Year's Eve 1990', 1992
Pascale Petit, 'My Father's Clothes', 1999

SEAM
Merryn Williams, 'Heading for the Heights', 1997

SOUTH
Pauline Hawkesworth, 'Meeting Place', *South* 20, October 1999

SMITHS KNOLL
Patricia Bishop, 'Woman Washing', No. 7

STAPLE
Julia Casterton, 'One Flesh', June 1999
Jenny Hamlett, 'The Therapist's Comment', *Staple* 35

SURVIVORS POETRY ANTHOLOGY, *Fresher Than Green, Brighter Than Orange* (ed. Lisa Boardman, Eamer O'Keeffe), 1999
Eamer O'Keeffe, 'Chords'

TABLA
Martha Kapos, 'The Pulse' (then titled 'The Dark House'), Summer, 1998. This poem is also included in *Tying the Song: A First Anthology from the Poetry School*, Enitharmon, 2000

TEESIDE WRITERS WORKSHOP ANTHOLOGY
Norah Hill, 'Dürer's Young Hare'

VIRAGO ANTHOLOGY, *Ain't I a Woman*, 1987
Katherine Gallagher, 'Distances'

WRITING WOMEN
Nadine Brummer, 'That Rank Bed', Volume 9, No. 1
Caroline Natzler, 'There', Volume 12, No. 3